A SUMMER
UP NORTH

A SUMMER UP NORTH

Henry Aaron and the
Legend of Eau Claire Baseball

with a foreword by
Allan H. (Bud) Selig

JERRY POLING

THE UNIVERSITY OF WISCONSIN PRESS

The University of Wisconsin Press
1930 Monroe Street
Madison, Wisconsin 53711

www.wisc.edu/wisconsinpress/

3 Henrietta Street
London WC2E 8LU, England

1   3   5   4   2

Printed in the United States of America

Library of Congress Cataloging-in-Publication Data
Poling, Jerry, 1958–
A summer up North : Henry Aaron and the legend of Eau Clair baseball
Jerry Poling ;
foreword by Allan H. (Bud) Selig.
pp.   cm.
Includes bibliographical references and index.
ISBN 0-299-18180-4 (cloth : alk. paper)
ISBN 0-299-18184-7 (pbk. : alk. paper)
1. Aaron, Hank, 1934– 2. Baseball players—United States—Biography.
3. Baseball—Wisconsin—Eau Claire—History—20th century.
4. Northern League of Professional Baseball. I. Title.
GV865.A25 P65   2002
796.357′092—dc21   2002003833

*For Henry Aaron and
the people of Eau Claire, Wisconsin*

CONTENTS

ILLUSTRATIONS

FOREWORD

For nearly fifty years, I have been privileged to be Henry Aaron's friend and one of his biggest fans. I watched him break into the majors in Milwaukee in 1954, sold him his first car, cheered him when he led the Braves to the 1957 World Series title, and proudly watched him break Babe Ruth's career home run record in Atlanta in 1974.

Then he came home to Milwaukee and, appropriately, finished his career with the Brewers in 1975 and 1976. He hit his final career home run at County Stadium.

No other person has made and seen as much Milwaukee baseball history as Henry. He was not only one of the greatest players ever, but for the last quarter-century he has been a role model and ambassador for the Milwaukee Brewers as well as for Major League Baseball.

Many people don't realize that his career predates Milwaukee baseball. He was signed in 1952 by the Boston Braves, before they moved to Milwaukee, and spent two years in the Braves' minor league system before reaching the majors.

Until I read *A Summer Up North,* I thought that I knew everything about Henry's career. It turns out that I knew little about one of the most important years of his life, 1952, when he made the leap from the Negro Leagues to the minor leagues.

Jerry Poling's very informative book about Aaron's first year in the minors in Eau Claire—a great baseball training ground for many Braves players—helped me understand how Henry Aaron bridged the cultural divide between growing up in the segregated South and playing in the North. That he did it in one important, sometimes trying, summer in Eau Claire gives me an even greater appreciation for one of my heroes.

Henry Aaron was one of the most disciplined athletes, mentally and physically, I ever knew. He also is one of the greatest people I have ever had the good fortune to know. *A Summer Up North* will help you appreciate why.

Allan H. (Bud) Selig
Commissioner of Baseball

ACKNOWLEDGMENTS

Many people, organizations, and businesses contributed their time, expertise, and resources to help make *A Summer Up North* possible. First, I must thank Henry Aaron, several of his 1952 Eau Claire Bears teammates, and other former Eau Claire Bears and Eau Claire Braves players for taking time to share their memories. Without fail, they gladly answered all my questions every time I called or met with them. I wouldn't have a clear picture of what it was like to play minor league baseball in the 1950s without them. Among them are Joe Torre and Bob Uecker, both of whom fit me into their schedules while they were at work. I'm especially thankful for many interviews with Ken Reitmeier, a 1952 Bears pitcher who candidly remembers events from fifty years ago as if they happened yesterday.

In addition to former players, city residents Mary Wall, Susan Hauck, Bill Anderson, and others helped me understand life in Eau Claire and Eau Claire baseball in the 1950s. As I neared the end of my research and writing, University of Wisconsin–Eau Claire professors Jim Oberly and John Hildebrand gave me valuable criticism and guidance.

Much of my research required access to private and public records. Thanks to my employer, the Eau Claire Press Company, publisher of the *Leader-Telegram,* for access to microfilm, Northern League records, and many historical photos. Thanks also to the Chippewa Valley Museum of Eau Claire; L. E. Phillips Memorial Library in Eau Claire; National Baseball Hall of Fame in Cooperstown, New York; Negro Leagues Baseball Museum in Kansas City, Missouri; Washington County Historical Society in Stillwater, Minnesota; Roger Maris Museum in Fargo, North Dakota; Stearns History Museum in Saint Cloud, Minnesota; Alexander Mitchell Library in Aberdeen, South Dakota; *Argus Leader* in Sioux Falls, South Dakota; Superior Public Library in Superior, Wisconsin; WTMJ Radio in Milwaukee; Milwaukee Brewers; Minnesota Twins; New York Yankees; Saint Paul Saints; Fargo-Moorhead RedHawks; and Duluth Dukes.

I am indebted to the University of Wisconsin Press for its support of writing about Wisconsin's history. I am especially thankful for the commitment of associate director Steve Salemson, who supported my work at every juncture.

Finally, I must thank my wife, Lynn, and my sons, Jerad and Matthew, for always encouraging me and showing interest in my work, although it often meant time away from them.

PROLOGUE

Much of Eau Claire, Wisconsin, was buzzing on August 17, 1994. Henry Aaron was on his way back to the city to unveil a bronze statue of himself. The local media previewed his return with such headlines as "Hammerin' Hank's Homecoming" and with live TV broadcasts in front of old Carson Park stadium, which was dressed up in red, white, and blue bunting. Reporters from around the state and nearby Minneapolis–Saint Paul also were on hand, thanks in part to a Major League Baseball strike that had idled not only the players but a legion of baseball writers. The statue was the baseball news of the day in the Upper Midwest.

Early that afternoon under partly sunny skies, Aaron stepped from a chartered plane at the Chippewa Valley Regional Airport in Eau Claire and was surprised to see more than a hundred children and adults waving to him. It seemed as if he wasn't expecting a crowd. The fans were carrying homemade signs and hoping for autographs. He smiled broadly and waved back. Although his arrival had been delayed for several hours because of a boarding mix-up in Atlanta, the fans still were waiting. As he left the airport, some people ran alongside and behind his limousine. He again smiled and waved back through the tinted glass.

Aaron had been straight-faced on the six-seat plane that took him from Minneapolis to Eau Claire, probably wondering if this would be another of those perfunctory duties a sports star must perform to maintain his image. But soon after deplaning he began to enjoy himself when he realized that his return to Eau Claire actually might be a day to remember.

He knew already that it was far different from his first visit to the city. Forty-two years earlier, in 1952, only a local sportswriter, Clell Buzzell, showed up at the airport to help the eighteen-year-old shortstop with his cardboard suitcase. "I was scared as hell," Aaron said, recalling his arrival as the new recruit on the city's Class C minor league baseball team. "I have to be very honest with you. I was just a little baby."

He wasn't just any new Eau Claire Bears player. He was supposed to be a phenom, one of the legion of young black players expected to follow on Jackie Robinson's heels and change baseball forever. He also was an eighteen-year-old from the Deep South on an extended trip away from home for the first time.

At a luncheon before the unveiling, Aaron told the audience what a big role Eau Claire had played in helping him overcome his apprehensions about being so far from home and in a mostly white city for the first time. "You made me realize that I had a dream, and the only thing that I could do was go out and play baseball as hard as I could play and my dream would be fulfilled. Once I got to the ballpark, all the fans opened their arms to me and accepted me and gave me their support and gave me things I never would have dreamed about."

Later that day, as reporters gathered around him at a news conference in a hotel, Aaron was asked about the significance of the three months he spent in Eau Claire in the scope of his twenty-three years in Major League Baseball. He replied, "Eau Claire was a great stepping-stone. If people had not accepted me in Eau Claire, my career would have stumbled a little bit. I don't know what would have happened to me in baseball."

That afternoon, as he approached the stadium, his eyes widened when he saw that cars were parked a mile away from the baseball field and people were streaming toward the covered statue. Known as a man who chooses his words wisely and makes his friends carefully, he obviously was moved by how many people were interested in seeing him when he said simply, "You've got quite a crowd here." He didn't know that he had been the talk of the city for several weeks. The estimated five thousand people—matching the biggest crowd since the stadium opened in 1937— surrounded the statue outside the stadium where he stroked his first professional base hit.

The Aaron fans were making a statement: Pro baseball had once been a great part of the city, and Henry Aaron was the greatest ever to play at Carson Park, one of the greatest ever to play anywhere. The people surrounded Aaron's limousine as it reached the stadium, barely leaving room for him to squeeze out. This wasn't Atlanta in April of 1974, when he broke Babe Ruth's home run record amidst death threats. He didn't need a bodyguard with a pistol as he did back then. He didn't seem worried or even uncomfortable as he plunged into the crowd and shook hands. People climbed trees and peered from the top row of grandstand seats to get better views.

Cameras, camcorders, and TV cameras were trained on him. In 1952 he had felt awkward when people in Eau Claire stared at his blackness, but this time he seemed invigorated. Now the people of Eau Claire were looking up to him. He wasn't just a hero; he was a baseball hero and a black hero. It was all he ever wanted. "I had goose bumps," he said later. "It was a blessed day for me. A lot of things happened to me in my twenty-three years as a ballplayer, but nothing touched me more than that day in Eau Claire. I'm not exaggerating. When you think about Eau Claire, this little town, to have that many people come out and that many kids, who have never seen me play, it was special. It was a tearjerker for me."

After a successful season in 1952 in Eau Claire, Aaron knew he could play baseball anywhere, such as Milwaukee, and realistically dream of going anywhere, even a place like the Baseball Hall of Fame.

But the people of Eau Claire never let him go. Aaron gradually became their symbol of a magical time in city history. The thirty-five thousand people who lived in Eau Claire in the 1950s—as well as the people from surrounding farm communities—were proud of their minor league baseball teams. Like hundreds of small cities across the nation, Eau Claire was one pulsing vein of a game that filled stadiums throughout the nation. Ever since the uncertain days of the Depression and then the hopeful days of the New Deal, the Eau Claire Bears and Eau Claire Braves had connected the city to Major League Baseball. From 1933 through 1962, by the tens of thousands each summer, Eau Claire fans faithfully climbed a sandstone bluff to the lovely stone stadium nestled in tall pine trees on an island in Half Moon Lake. There they watched their team, their Major League prospects, battle the athletic heroes of some other Northern League town. No matter what was happening in the United States or around the world, they knew they could count on a good baseball game.

They counted on the American dream too. They saw young men who someday would be playing for Milwaukee, Saint Louis, Cleveland, Philadelphia, New York, or Chicago, men who someday would be in the World Series. Or in the Hall of Fame. They believed it, and they saw it happen. Dreams came true in America, even in hard times.

Baseball in those days—before, during, and after Henry Aaron—certainly made Eau Claire a more exciting place to live. Once known as the Sawdust City, for its lumberjacks and lumber mills in the late 1800s, later on it produced automobile tires, tissue paper, disposable diapers, horseradish, beer, and computer products. It's not a city where big news happens but a place where life seems to roll along happily, sometimes a little behind the times but thankful for it, especially when it comes to the litany of crimes elsewhere that seldom occur in Eau Claire. While most murders in big cities no longer make headlines, any murder within a fifty-mile radius would have led newscasts and dominated headlines in Eau Claire at the start of the twenty-first century.

Along with Henry Aaron and lumbering, Eau Claire's legacy includes the unexciting subject of milk. Not only is Eau Claire in the central part of the state known as America's Dairyland, but it happens to be the epicenter of pricing for whole, skim, 2 percent, and 1 percent milk. In the 1930s, the federal government determined that Eau Claire was the geographic center of the nation's dairy industry. Wishing to encourage milk production in areas other than the Midwest, it decided to base federal price supports on the distance of a milking region from Eau Claire. Consequently Eau Claire has been a home field of sorts for cows as well as minor league baseball since 1933. It is famous among farm organizations but few others. Whenever dairy farms begin to fail because of low milk prices—an almost annual adversity—the city makes national news as farmers and congressmen and senators wonder why something hasn't been done with the antiquated federal milk pricing policy.

On his way to fame and fortune, Henry Aaron couldn't have landed in a better city than Eau Claire if he wanted to experience Middle America. Eau Claire has a middle-of-the-road feel for good reason. At almost forty-five degrees north latitude, the city is about halfway between the equator and the North Pole; at just over ninety degrees longitude, it is about halfway around the western hemisphere. Furthermore, the city is near the nation's middle border, the Mississippi River. Eau Claire is a middle-class midwestern town that usually lands in the middle of lists of desirable metropolitan areas, according to *Places Rated Almanac*. It may not be an exciting place, but it's safe, scenic, and home to about sixty thousand people.

Few famous people grew up in Eau Claire or have lived there. Mostly the city has had brushes with fame. Young novelist F. Scott Fitzgerald used to glance out the train window at Eau Claire en route from Princeton University in New Jersey to his home in Saint Paul; he once used a pitiful Eau Claire character in a short story, "Bernice Bobs Her Hair." The story didn't win him any awards, but he was busy working on the 1920 classic *This Side of Paradise* at the time so he can be excused if it wasn't his best piece. Twin sisters Ann Landers and Abigail Van Buren lived in Eau Claire from the mid-1940s to mid-1950s, but they hadn't begun solving people's problems as newspaper columnists. (What advice would they have given Henry Aaron about feeling uncomfortable in a place that was all white?) In Eau Claire, they were housewives Esther "Eppie" Lederer (Ann) and Pauline "Popo" Phillips (Abigail). Esther also tested her listening skills as a volunteer at Luther Hospital near Carson Park and as chair of the Eau Claire County Democratic Party, a position that the witch-hunting politics of Republican Senator Joe McCarthy inflamed her to run for.

Eau Claire often has been close enough to touch great people. Budding musician Buddy Holly and his troupe played "Peggy Sue" at Fournier's Dance Hall—now long gone—along the Chippewa River on January 26, 1959, one week before his fatal plane crash in an Iowa cornfield. Martin Luther King Jr. spoke at the university in 1962, one year before his "I Have a Dream" speech in Washington. Many presidential candidates have visited the city, but no sitting president has ever stopped. In November of 1992, President George Bush passed near Eau Claire, stopping by train in Chippewa Falls, where he received the news from his pollster that he would not be reelected. President Taft once stayed overnight in Eau Claire—after he no longer was president. Presidents McKinley and Hoover didn't even get off the train when they passed through. Vice President Richard Nixon gave a speech in Eau Claire in 1958 and visited several more times in the 1960s before he became president. Theodore Roosevelt reportedly lived in Eau Claire at the turn of the century, but he wasn't *the* Theodore Roosevelt, just a first cousin of the president. Franklin Roosevelt's wife, Eleanor, gave a speech in Eau Claire on United Nations Day in 1954, but she no longer was first lady.

Baseball players have long been Eau Claire's connection to fame, but even these men weren't famous when they lived in Eau Claire. The city had its first professional, or paid, players in 1884, the year of the first World Series. The earliest protégé to become famous was Burleigh Grimes, who threw the first of his famous spitballs in Eau Claire in 1912 and later became a World Series hero, a teammate of Babe Ruth, and a member of the Baseball Hall of Fame. Other Eau Claire minor leaguers turned into Major League all-stars and were teammates of baseball immortals like Jackie Robinson, Willie Mays, and even the midget Eddie Gaedel.

For two decades after he played in Eau Claire, Henry Aaron was just another in a long line of successful major leaguers that the city called its own. Then in 1974 he broke Babe Ruth's home run record. Aaron became a hero to the nation. Everyone in the world was talking about him, Presidents Nixon and Ford, comedian Flip Wilson, civil rights activists Jesse Jackson and Andrew Young, Sammy Davis Jr., and even the baseball-loving Japanese. Muhammad Ali proclaimed in his best raspy voice that Aaron was the greatest. Aaron became much bigger even than baseball, a symbol of American success, a symbol of black success, and unfortunately at times a symbol of America's slow progress in race relations. The story of Aaron's breaking the record was as much about the racist hate mail he received as it was about his achievement, as much about being black as it was about being successful.

Over the years, Eau Claire quietly embraced Aaron as its hero. It didn't matter that Aaron lived in Eau Claire for just one summer. It didn't matter that Aaron was one of the first black players in city history (Billy Bruton came first in 1950 followed by Horace Garner in 1951). It didn't matter that Aaron—and two of his 1952 teammates—were black and Eau Claire was virtually all white. Black wasn't the issue. Eau Claire gave him his start, his first place to play in the minor leagues, and the city quietly celebrated that fact every time Aaron made history.

As he grew famous, people who lived in Eau Claire in 1952 began to remember in detail the days of the minor leagues. If relatives came to town and wanted to know something unique about Eau Claire, their hosts often would drive them by the stadium and tell the Aaron story. City residents began to remember his first hit, his first home runs, playing cards with him at the YMCA, serving him at restaurants or cooking him meals and trying to make him feel at home when he was eighteen and far from Mobile, Alabama. An Aaron scholarship fund was started at the University of Wisconsin–Eau Claire. He became an adopted son, a local legend.

I was born in Eau Claire in 1958 in a hospital just across Half Moon Lake from Carson Park, where the Eau Claire Braves played minor league baseball (the name was changed from Bears in 1954). It was an off year. That summer the team won sixty-five games and lost fifty-six, finishing in fifth place in the Class C Northern League, despite having the league's leading hitter, Manuel Jimenez, who batted .340. The team also had a muscular first baseman with an impressive lineage, Tommie Aaron (Henry's younger brother), and a promising pitcher, Tony Cloninger. All three were future major leaguers. The Braves had done better. In twenty-five previous seasons, they had twenty-one winning seasons and five minor league pennants.

I never knew the Eau Claire Bears or Braves. By the time I was four years old, in 1962, they were playing their final games a half-mile from my house. By the time I was seven, the Major League team that they were affiliated with, the Milwaukee Braves, had packed up the toothy Indian logo and hatchet, Eddie Mathews, and Henry Aaron and left Wisconsin for Atlanta, Georgia.

When I was nine, my family left Eau Claire too. But I returned at age twenty-four to make Eau Claire my home again. I went to work for the *Eau Claire Leader-Telegram,* writing, editing, and researching sports and news stories. I read all I could about the city's history. On August 17, 1994, I saw a side of Eau Claire that I never knew, the Eau Claire that once loved pro baseball. The reason: It was Henry Aaron Day in Eau Claire. When the five thousand souls surrounded Aaron on a grassy plaza outside Carson Park stadium, when they cheered long and loud as he pulled a royal blue cloth off a bronze bust of himself as a skinny teenager, when they pressed in close for autographs and listened intently to his speeches, then I knew. Not only was I born too late to see Henry Aaron play in Eau Claire, but I missed some of the best days of the 150-year-old city that I call home.

I was born too late to see Henry Aaron, his brother Tommie, Billy Bruton, Wes Covington, Joe Torre, Bob Uecker, Tony Cloninger, Rico Carty, Wes Westrum, Andy Pafko, Burleigh Grimes, or any of the young

Eau Claire prospects before they became great. Born too late to see the spirit of the growing city reflected in its support of its baseball teams.

So I began to go back in time and listen to a baseball story told by old news clippings, microfilm, photographs, ex-ballplayers, and longtime city residents who spoke with warm smiles about the good days when "everybody" in town went to the ball games, when the talk on the streets after a game was all about the big hits, the key plays, the pennant race, the newest player in town.

The story of baseball in Eau Claire is nearly as old as the city. In many ways, it mirrors the history of American baseball.

A SUMMER
UP NORTH

chapter 1

NORTH TO THE
NORTHERN LEAGUE

I t's a long way from down the bay, as they say on the Gulf Coast in
Mobile, Alabama, to the Chippewa River in Eau Claire, Wisconsin.
In 1952, the year he turned eighteen, Henry Aaron made a round trip
and realized one thing: He was good enough to play pro baseball. Before
then, he didn't know. Metaphorically speaking, 1952 was Henry Aaron's
first home run, a hit all the way across the country, a success that would
foreshadow the extent of his fame in the coming years.

Because Aaron grew up in Mobile, Mobile and not Eau Claire should
probably get most of the credit for sending him to the Major Leagues.
Mobile must have had good gumbo, good water, or good blood lines
because it also was the hometown of Satchel Paige, Billy Williams, Willie
McCovey, Ozzie Smith—all Hall of Famers as well—and a few other
pretty good major leaguers: Amos Otis, Tommie Agee, Cleon Jones. But
Mobile—a former slave trading post and the last major city in the
Confederacy to fall during the Civil War—was segregated and not an
easy place for a black ballplayer to get noticed. Brothers Frank and Milt
Bolling, who became major leaguers in the 1950s and 1960s, grew up near
some of these black future baseball stars. Yet they had no idea who their
neighbors were because they lived on the other side of the tracks. Milt,
who played for the Boston Braves in the early 1950s, was once asked if
he knew Henry Aaron. "Well, it turns out he only lived a few blocks from
me. We lived a block and a half this side of the railroad tracks, Hank
Aaron lived maybe a block and a half on the other side. Never heard of

him, and he's only a year younger than I am," Bolling said in Larry Moffi's *This Side of Cooperstown.*

When Aaron began playing baseball with his father, brothers, and friends in a vacant neighborhood lot in Mobile, hitting bottle caps with a broomstick, he dreamed of being Jackie Robinson. Born February 5, 1934, Aaron had just turned thirteen when Robinson broke Major League Baseball's color barrier with the Brooklyn Dodgers in April 1947. On that day, Robinson crossed the railroad tracks for blacks everywhere. The event stirred big ideas in the adolescent Aaron. "When Jackie Robinson got that opportunity, every black person around the country said, 'Hey, we've got a chance now.' I knew if I played well I had a chance to get out of Mobile," Aaron said. "Without Jackie Robinson, there wouldn't have been any Hank Aaron."

By the spring of 1952 Aaron was out of Mobile. In the summer of 1951 he had been playing shortstop on Sundays with a semipro team in Mobile, the Black Bears. The owner of the Black Bears knew the owner of the traveling Indianapolis Clowns, Syd Pollock, who promptly came to Mobile to get a look at young Henry. Pollock liked what he saw and said he would send him a contract the next spring. Aaron turned eighteen in February of 1952 but was still in high school when he apprehensively got on a train with two dollars, two pairs of pants, and two sandwiches and left for spring training with the Clowns in Winston-Salem, North Carolina. He was on his own for the first time, and more than once he thought about getting off the train and going back home.

As it turned out, Aaron was catching one of the last trains to the Negro Leagues. The Negro National League folded in 1948 after Robinson and other stars went to the majors, and the Clowns were the only drawing card left in the Negro American League, which was down to six teams and fading fast. The Clowns originated in the 1930s in Miami as the Ethiopian Clowns. Their crowd-pleasing antics, such as playing shadow-ball and throwing confetti on the fans, eventually were emulated by the Harlem Globetrotters basketball team. Goose Tatum played on the Clowns and the Globetrotters. Jesse Owens played for the Clowns in the 1930s and Satchel Paige in the 1960s.

Some Negro League players in the 1940s thought the Clowns gave the league a bad reputation. The Clowns had a juggler, a contortionist, a midget, and an ambidextrous pitcher, Double Duty Green. Their acts

Hank Aaron

In the spring of 1952 Henry Aaron's hitting drew the attention
of Major League scouts when he played for the Indianapolis Clowns
in the Negro Leagues. He was signed by the Boston Braves and
sent to Wisconsin to play for the Eau Claire Bears.

(Photo courtesy of Negro Leagues Baseball Museum)

included firecrackers, cherry bombs, and a player dressed in drag. But they toned down their routines and became a baseball team first. A few Clowns in 1952, like Richard "King" Tut, with a glove the size of an elephant's ear, and Spec Bebop, his four-feet-six-inch sidekick, still did some clowning but only in the seventh inning. No one laughed at Aaron, even though teammates nicknamed him Pork Chops (for his favorite food) and Little Brother.

In 1952 Sherwood Brewer was playing for the Kansas City Monarchs of the Negro Leagues. He had played with the Clowns in the late 1940s and was a four-time All-Star at four positions—third base, shortstop, second base, and outfield. He remembers first encountering Aaron one day when the Monarchs played the Clowns in Little Rock, Arkansas. "[Aaron] was sitting on the bench just before the game started, and he said to [Clowns manager] Buster Haywood, 'This is a small ballpark.' Here was this kid saying this. Haywood said, 'What did you say?' Aaron said, 'This is a small park.'" Neither Haywood nor Brewer was sure why the small, inexperienced Aaron would say that about a Major League–size field. Until the game began. "Aaron hit two over the scoreboard that day," Brewer said with a chuckle.

As the Clowns traveled down the East Coast and through the South in April and May of 1952—Aaron never did play in Indianapolis—it soon became apparent that Aaron wasn't just another skinny kid trying to earn $200 a month to send home. He was young enough and good enough to escape the Negro Leagues, unlike many of the aging players who, like the league itself, were on their last legs. Aaron began to hit line drives off the walls, his batting average shot up over .400, and Pollock could smell a cash sale. He mentioned Aaron in the postscript of a letter he sent to the Braves scouting director. The Clowns owned Aaron as a baseball player and could sell him to the highest bidder.

The Boston (soon-to-be Milwaukee) Braves sent scout Dewey Griggs to investigate Aaron. Although Aaron batted cross-handed—Griggs corrected Aaron in late May—Griggs saw unlimited potential. He sent a letter to the Braves on May 25, 1952, saying that Aaron "could be the answer." The Braves—who had lost Willie Mays to the Giants—offered Pollock $10,000 for a cash sale and offered Aaron $350 a month salary in the minor leagues. The New York Giants and the New York Yankees also made contract offers to Aaron. But Philadelphia scout Judy Johnson, the great

Negro Leaguer, couldn't get the Athletics to offer the Clowns even $3,500 cash for Aaron.

When the bidding closed, the Giants had offered Aaron $100 a month less than the Braves, misspelled his name "Arron" on a telegram, and missed their man. The Braves almost missed their man too. Scouting director John Mullen sent the offer by telegram to the Clowns only ten minutes before their contract option on Aaron expired. In an article in the *Saturday Evening Post* on August 25, 1956, Braves general manager John Quinn recalled the signing of Aaron: "Remember, we were not rich back there in 1952. Ten thousand dollars was a good deal of money to us that year. We had drawn badly in 1951 in Boston, and we were having it even rougher in 1952."

After the sale was completed, Aaron played two more weeks with the Clowns, winding up with a game at Comiskey Park in Chicago on June 8. He then took a train to Milwaukee and flew to Eau Claire four days later.

Aaron was about to become part of a decades-old system—the minor leagues—but one that had been invigorated since the war. The minor leagues formed in the 1920s and reached their peak in the late 1940s and early 1950s, after men returned from World War II. Each year during that time, nearly ten thousand men on three to four hundred teams were trying to make the Major Leagues.

In 1952, 324 teams played in forty-three leagues (although only half the leagues were affiliated with the majors). The Boston Braves alone had twelve farm teams playing in twelve leagues. Far from Mobile as it was, Eau Claire was closest to home for Aaron among the Braves' three Class C teams. Teams ranged from Class D to Class AAA. In Class C, Aaron could have been sent to Braves teams in Quebec, Canada, in the Provincial League or Ventura, California, in the California League. Chances are he came to Eau Claire because the Northern League had a reputation for being the best in its class in the country, equivalent almost to a Class A level, some observers thought.

Still, the career of one of America's greatest athletes was off to a humble start. After all, it was Class C ball, second to lowest in the minors and five steps down the ladder from the majors. Aaron arrived with his clothes in a cardboard suitcase, a gift from the not-so-generous owner of the Clowns. He had no signing bonus and no guaranteed contract. He would

be playing Upper Midwest baseball. The league that season included the
Eau Claire (Wisconsin) Bears, Superior (Wisconsin) Blues, the Duluth
(Minnesota) Dukes, the Fargo-Moorhead (North Dakota–Minnesota)
Twins, the Grand Forks (North Dakota) Chiefs, the Aberdeen (South
Dakota) Pheasants, the Sioux Falls (South Dakota) Canaries, and the
Saint Cloud (Minnesota) Rox.

If the Braves didn't like Aaron after thirty days, he would be headed
back to Mobile or back to the Clowns, wherever they were. Six years
earlier, Jackie Robinson received a $3,500 signing bonus, and three years
earlier Willie Mays received a $15,000 signing offer from the Giants
when they bought him from the Birmingham (Alabama) Black Barons.
Right from the start, it seemed, people didn't think Aaron was as good
as Robinson or Mays. If Aaron was highly regarded—and it seems he
was—Major League owners weren't letting on. Most likely the Braves
didn't have to give Aaron a bonus because he was eighteen, unknown,
and untried. He was a high school kid who might break records or—like
so many other promising players—might never break into the majors.

The North Central Airlines ride to Eau Claire was the first flying experience of Aaron's life. If the bumpy airplane ride didn't shake him up
enough, Aaron's first view of Eau Claire probably did. The city must have
seemed as if it was in another country. Eau Claire had thirty-five thousand
people; Mobile had that many shipyard workers. It certainly was a different color. Eau Claire never had to worry about segregation since there
was no one to segregate, except maybe the stoic German Lutherans from
the Scandinavian Lutherans or any Lutherans from the Roman Catholics.
The Ku Klux Klan was a presence in the area in the 1920s, but its target
was not blacks, because there were few, but Catholics and Jews.

Aaron was greeted at the north side airport by thirty-four-year-old
Clell "Buzz" Buzzell, a small-framed, unimposing, brown-haired man
with glasses who was the sports editor of the local newspaper. The unassuming Buzzell was a big supporter of the local baseball team. Buzzell
not only covered the Bears' games but also, in those days before journalism ethics was a big issue, was their official scorer and in charge of finding
housing for the players. With Aaron in the passenger seat of his 1949
Chevrolet, Buzzell drove east of Eau Claire several miles to his white,
two-story country house. They went up the long driveway toward the
big front porch and went inside. Aaron was farther away from home than

he'd ever been and was standing in the living room of a white couple's home. Until that moment, he had lived exclusively in an African American world—black schools, black neighborhood, black baseball teams. Bigotry and segregation had closed off everything that was white. At that moment, at the Buzzells' front door, he crossed over the threshhold into a new world, one that he would steadfastly help change in the decades to come with his accomplishments on the baseball field and his role off the field as a black leader.

On June 12, 1952, Aaron was simply an innocent teenager. Buzzell, proud of his newspaper and community work, had stopped home to let his wife, Joyce, meet the Bears' newest player. The introduction might have been a pleasure for Joyce but not for Aaron. Seeing the scared, skinny young man in her living room, Joyce thought he was fourteen or fifteen years old and feeling out-of-place. She felt sorry for him. "He was shaking," Joyce said of Aaron. "He had never been in a white person's home before."

Although he didn't know it at the time, that meeting was the beginning of a long-lasting relationship. Before the summer was over, Aaron would go to the Buzzells for dinner several times and play with their children. Almost fifty years later, he would call Joyce Buzzell and offer his condolences when Clell died.

According to the 1950 U.S. Census, Eau Claire had only twenty-seven nonwhites, seven of whom were black. Aaron would be one of three black players on the Bears team. There were more black people in his house back home. Outside of the ballpark, he saw only one other black person in Eau Claire that summer.

A lack of diversity was common in most Wisconsin cities then. Although the state's black population grew from twelve thousand in 1940 to twenty-eight thousand in 1950 and seventy-four thousand in 1960, most lived in southeastern Wisconsin in and around Milwaukee. Even in 1960, only two counties outside of the southeast had more than a hundred black residents, and such cities as Appleton, Stevens Point, Green Bay, and Oshkosh had only a handful. "The result was that most white people in Wisconsin had no contact whatsoever with Negroes in school, at work, or through church and other organized activities. Consequently, they had no opportunity within their own communities to test at first hand the widely held white stereotypes about Negroes," writes William F. Thompson in

The History of Wisconsin: Continuity and Change, 1940–1965. The Wisconsin Fair Employment Act in 1945 was passed to prevent discrimination in hiring "because of race, color, creed, national origin or ancestry," but it was years before the law had an impact. Milwaukee breweries didn't begin hiring blacks until 1950. Milwaukee hired its first black teacher in 1951, and a major Milwaukee department store hired the first black full-time salesperson in 1952, the same year Aaron debuted in Eau Claire.

Eau Claire's ethnic makeup has changed little. After the 1980 census showed only 130 black residents in the city, *Time* magazine called it the whitest metropolitan area in the United States. That number rose to 211 in 1990 and 429 in 2000. In the 1980s and 1990s, the city became much more diverse with an influx of several thousand southeast Asians—Hmong—who fled Communist oppression after the Vietnam War.

In the summer of 1952 Aaron was thrust into a white world. He was going to eat, travel, socialize, play with, and be managed and admired by white people for the first time in his life. It was his indoctrination to the culture of northern white people, and he would find out whether they were as disrespecting of blacks as the southern whites.

It wasn't the only life lesson he would learn in Eau Claire. He would also discover how to succeed when lonely and when all eyes were on him, an ability that he would need twenty-two years later when he closed in on Babe Ruth's career home run record.

The second stop of Aaron's first day in Eau Claire was the Eau Claire Young Men's Christian Association at 101 South Farwell Street where he would live that summer. It was located in the city's pretty but modest downtown, which was three streets wide and a mile long. The downtown is positioned below a wooded bluff and between the perpendicular Chippewa and Eau Claire rivers, which merge in the heart of the city. Aaron and Buzzell drove past the city's biggest employer, U.S. Rubber, whose forty-four hundred workers made about twenty thousand tires a day in a quarter-mile long red brick factory. They drove across the Eau Claire River past the Oldsmobile dealer with the hot new Rocket 88 on the lot, past Western Union Telegraph, and past the building that housed the State theater and bowling alley.

The YMCA was on a prominent corner downtown on Farwell Street. Next door to the south were the Carnegie library and stately city hall, built in 1903 and 1916. Both were constructed of buff Bedford limestone, their entrances framed by four Corinthian columns. City hall is a replica of the Petit Trianon in Versailles, France, built by King Louis XVI. To the north was the red brick Hobbs Supply, a hardware wholesaler. Across the street were the Union bus depot and a gas station. Behind the YMCA was the Soo Line train station, and a few blocks north was the Chicago, Saint Paul, Minneapolis and Omaha railroad depot. The depot was an 1893 Richardsonian Romanesque building of Lake Superior brownstone, the same rock used in famous New York City and Chicago buildings. Between the YMCA and the depot was Sacred Heart Church, which had twin Romanesque Revival towers and two white Latin crosses that hung over the city.

Henry Aaron rented a room at the YMCA in downtown Eau Claire while playing for the Bears in 1952. He and teammates usually walked from the YMCA to their games at Carson Park stadium.

(Photo courtesy of Chippewa Valley Museum, Eau Claire, Wisconsin)

One block away from the YMCA and perched on a hillside was Eau Claire High School, a 1925 three-story brick building in collegiate Gothic style with a medieval-style entrance. Graduation ceremonies had taken place only a few days before Aaron arrived. Had he not left home for the Clowns, Aaron may have been in Mobile that day with a high school diploma in his hands.

Near the YMCA were the most and least elegant retail shops in town— Samuelson's Department Store and Woolworth's—and dozens of specialty shops that were all open to Aaron, many, in fact, that would welcome him. Eau Claire had no white and black shopping areas, no white and black sides of the tracks, no white and black drinking fountains. But it did have residents who would stare, unaccustomed to seeing a black person. For the first time in his life, Aaron could go where he pleased and do what he pleased—if he had the nerve.

Eau Claire probably wouldn't have noticed anyway, but the civil rights movement hadn't begun in earnest. In 1952, ten of the sixteen Major League teams still had not fielded a black player, and it would be another seven years before they all would come around. It was 1954 before the Supreme Court ruled to integrate schools in *Brown v. Board of Education* and 1957 before Congress passed the first Civil Rights Act since 1875. It was 1964 before a law guaranteed that black players could stay in the same hotels and eat at the same restaurants as their white teammates. Aaron was on a personal mission that someday would be symbolic for blacks, but in 1952 he had only one goal: to prove that he could play professional baseball.

In 1952, blacks were still proving they were as good as whites. At the YMCA in Eau Claire, on the early summer days of June in northern Wisconsin, on the baseball field, and in the community for the first time Aaron would test his limits as a baseball player and as an American.

The four-story YMCA had been built of red brick and sandstone and was dedicated by Wisconsin Governor Francis McGovern before a crowd of fifteen thousand in 1911. It was the city's male gathering place, the center for athletics, recreation, banquets, and other social functions, such as weekly Toastmasters meetings. A county history book describes the facility as "the social center of the city among the men's organizations. . . . The homelike atmosphere and moral tone of the building cannot help but uplift everyone coming in contact with it." It was a men's club—no facilities were built for women—as evidenced by the fact that all swimming in the early years was done in the nude.

When Aaron arrived the YMCA was not a bustling place. After spending the past five winter months indoors, many of its fourteen hundred members were outside—taking walks, playing baseball, mowing lawns, or fishing, boating, or swimming in the rivers and lakes. After months on the road with the nomadic Clowns, Aaron must have found the quiet, sturdy YMCA to be a sanctuary, even if it was in a white city. The YMCA had fifty rooms for rent at the modest price of one dollar a day, a perfect situation for young ballplayers like Aaron who didn't know how long they'd be in town. In addition, the players could hang out with other athletes, play pool or basketball, swim, or lounge in the hotel-like lobby, which had tables for chess or card games, easy chairs, and a brick fireplace. Luckily for the shy Aaron, the YMCA was clean and the rooms were big. The manager was Clayton Anderson, a former Air Force instructor and a fatherly type who kicked people out for two weeks if they were caught swearing. One of the YMCA's program directors was Vic Johnson, a former Major League pitcher who shut out the New York Yankees and Joe DiMaggio in 1945. The YMCA was a hangout for jocks, though no one called them that back then. Aaron had a telephone in his room and, thanks to his mother, an Oceanic radio on which he listened to Chicago Cubs games in the afternoon before the Bears games at night. Aaron had to like hearing the voice of the Cubs, Bert Wilson, calling out home runs by northside slugger Henry John Sauer, who hit 37 homers and drove home 121 runs in 1952 to lead the National League in both categories. Sauer's nickname had a nice ring: Hammerin' Hank. Historically, the YMCA was the right place for Aaron, the last major star to come out of the Negro Leagues. In 1920 the Negro Leagues were founded at a meeting at a YMCA in Kansas City, Missouri.

After Buzzell dropped him off and he checked into the YMCA, Aaron went out to Carson Park for the first time. The Bears, facing the Saint Cloud Rox, had just returned home after a six-day road trip in South Dakota, playing in Aberdeen and Sioux Falls. Players staying at the YMCA usually walked the 1.3 miles to Carson Park stadium, sometimes cutting through the brick and stone buildings of downtown—the grand three-story Elks Club lodge and American National Bank and Trust, the commercial gothic Kline's Department Store, Badger theater, Sears. In their typical attire—dress slacks and dress shirt—players strode across the trussed gray-steel Grand Avenue bridge that spanned the Chippewa River; past the Salvation Army, Gavin's Standard gas station, Goodlove's Market, Mahogany Bar, and Tan Top Bakery; past the arching stained-glass windows and eleven bells of Grace Lutheran Church, and, on the opposite side of the street, construction of the new $850,000 county courthouse and jail. Then they passed several blocks of turn-of-the-century two-story homes, many with wraparound front porches a few feet from the Grand Avenue sidewalks. One of the homes was a Queen Anne style built by Christian Reinhard, who emigrated from Germany in 1841 and built his dream home in 1873—shortly after the first-ever baseball games were played in Eau Claire—on one of the city's finest streets. The Bears marched past Reinhard's still-proud two-story home straight west to a two-lane causeway over Half Moon Lake and up a winding set of stone steps to the fifteen-year-old beige sandstone stadium. That night Aaron saw his Bears defeat the Saint Cloud Rox, 5–2, behind the pitching of Gordon Roach, a six-feet-four Canadian with a distinctly northern nickname, Moose.

The baseball stadium was part of a large wooded park, the central park of Eau Claire, which included a football field, softball fields, tennis courts, playgrounds, and picnic areas, all sitting on a low bluff surrounded by the lake. Construction of Carson Park stadium had begun at the height of the Depression, in 1935, and was funded by and considered a major project by President Franklin Roosevelt's Works Progress Administration. The WPA paid unskilled laborers forty-eight dollars a month. More than three thousand pine tree stumps had to be removed to lay out the fields. Sandstone blocks for the grandstand were trucked in from the Dunnville quarry twenty-five miles downriver, the same quarry that had supplied blocks for Saint Thomas Episcopal Church in New York.

The stadium and park were named for the man who donated the land to the city for a park, William Carson, a prominent lumberman and banker and a friend of President Grover Cleveland. The park had opened to the public beginning in 1915 with a city picnic. During the late 1800s the horseshoe-shaped island had been used as a lumber camp and sawmill. Men like Carson made their fortunes (he was one of sixty-four millionaires in Wisconsin in 1892) sawing up hard, virgin white pine from northern

Wisconsin. The prized logs, which grew ramrod straight a hundred feet or more, were floated down the Chippewa River to Eau Claire and other sawmill cities.

In 1937, Carson Park was ready for baseball. The cost was $60,000, and that included the football stadium and field and three tennis courts. The baseball stadium, however, accounted for $50,000 of the $60,000 expense. The city's share of that was $25,000.

Seating at the baseball stadium was 1,500, plus 775 on portable wooden bleachers, but more than 3,000 fans turned out for the first game—the Bears versus the Superior Blues—at 3 P.M. Tuesday, May 4, 1937. City hall closed at 2 P.M. for the game. In attendance was Wisconsin Governor Philip La Follette, who said prophetically, "There is something in this world besides making money, and right here you have an athletic layout that will serve the boys and girls of your city for generations to come." The stadium was trumpeted in the news with stories and photos. "Eau Claire's new baseball plant at Carson Park is pronounced by those who

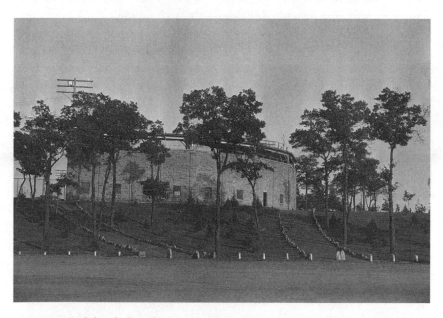

Carson Park baseball stadium as it appeared in 1937, the year it opened. It was built during the Depression as a Works Progress Administration project.
(Photo courtesy of the *Eau Claire Leader-Telegram*)

have had occasion to see such plants all over the country one of the finest in the land."

The stadium was dedicated June 1, 1937, with an exhibition game against the Class AAA Minneapolis Millers. An estimated five thousand people—the biggest baseball crowd in city history—saw the contest, which also was the stadium's first game played under lights. When the lights went on at 8 P.M., the beams from eleven poles flooded the field with light equal to forty-eight candles per square foot. Officials didn't start the game until 8:45, waiting for sunset to get the full effect of the lights. The Millers had defeated the Saint Paul Saints earlier that day in a league game, then hopped on a bus and headed for Eau Claire. The Millers lineup included Bill Dickey, a catcher who later starred for the New York Yankees and made the Hall of Fame (which was established in Cooperstown, New York, that year). A seventh-inning inside-the-park home run by Ode Barnett with Frank Scalise on base gave the Bears a 2–0 lead, but the Millers rallied for a 6–2 victory.

The new park was a hit. A total of forty thousand people attended games in 1937. The mood of the nation was changing. Eau Claire's first radio station went on the air that year. The Depression was letting up, and people were humming "Happy Days Are Here Again" on their way across the lake to the stadium, which symbolized a sort of bedrock faith in the country's future.

The stadium and its optimistic ballplayers became the city's symbols of hope and progress in an otherwise pessimistic time. Yet the stadium wasn't just a symbol—it was a fine place to play and watch a ball game. With the stadium facing east, the afternoon sun sets over Carson Park's third-base side on summer evenings, keeping fans cool and giving only the right fielder a few innings of sun problems. "The arrangement of the diamond was patterned after the Cubs [Wrigley Field] in Chicago with respect to the afternoon sun and in other ways," said Johnny Mostil, the former White Sox All-Star who was the Bears' first manager. "It's one of the best parks I've ever seen." The grandstand has five thick sandstone sides that form a C behind home plate, fourteen rows of seats, and many obstructed views. Thirty metal beams prop up the pitched roof, which starts about six feet above the top of the back wall and ends thirty-some feet above the box seats. The stadium has the spartan look and feel of a clapboard garage that would have housed a 1930s Ford. It is 320 feet down the left field line to the football field, 388 to center, and 312 to right, roughly the dimensions and shape of old Crosley Field in Cincinnati, where Aaron would hit some of his first Major League home runs.

The day had been a long one for Aaron, and when he went to bed at the YMCA he probably was hoping for a good night's sleep. At 4:30 A.M., however, a thunderstorm with forty-five mile-per-hour winds hit the city, dumping more than an inch of rain, uprooting trees in the area of the YMCA, scattering branches on many streets, and blowing down a barn outside the city. Electrical service was out to much of Eau Claire after trees fell on power lines. It was the morning of Friday, June 13.

That day, Buzzell filed a short story on the second sports page of the *Daily Telegram*, the sister to the morning *Leader*. "One new player arrived Thursday night and two more are due here within the next three days as the Eau Claire Bears continued to bring in replacements to strengthen their bid for honors in the 1952 Northern League. Henry Aaron, the young Negro shortstop who was batting .467 with the Indianapolis Clowns, arrived Thursday and will go on the active list soon. He was signed as a bonus player by the parent Boston Braves." Aaron laughed years later when he heard himself referred to as a bonus player, recalling that his only bonus for signing was his cardboard suitcase, which disintegrated one day in an Eau Claire rainstorm. Also, he remembered his batting average had dropped below .400 before he left the Clowns.

Friday the thirteenth brought more rain to Eau Claire, postponing the night game against Saint Cloud. Maybe Aaron caught a movie a half-block away at the State theater, whose marquee was visible from the front of the YMCA. The State was showing the technicolor feature *David and Bathsheba* starring Gregory Peck and Susan Hayward, followed at 11:30 P.M. by a Friday the thirteenth double feature, *The Black Cat* with Basil Rathbone and *Ghosts on the Loose*.

On Saturday, June 14, Aaron's once-small world began to expand. In Eau Claire, Aaron signed a four-page document that made him the property of the Boston Braves, one of the most storied teams in baseball history (they began playing in the National League in 1876), and the Eau Claire Bears. The Uniform Player Contract of the National Association of Professional Baseball Leagues was co-signed by Walter J. Brock, business manager of the Bears. Aaron listed his home address as 2010 Edward

Avenue, Mobile, Alabama. The agreement gave Aaron $350 a month during the season—$200 a month from the Bears and $150 a month from Evansville, Indiana, of the Class B Three-I League. For an eighteen-year-old who was almost penniless, the money must have looked like a windfall—even if it was for only three months. The wage was better than most players were making in the Northern League, where the team salary cap for the season was $3,400. With a roster limit of seventeen, that meant the average salary was $200 a month, which is probably why Aaron received his other $150 a month from Evansville. Aaron's salary also was better than most people were making in Wisconsin. The average manufacturing wage in Eau Claire in 1952, the best in the state, was $325 a month.

Aaron's contract was signed later by the president of the NAPBL and by Herman D. White, the Northern League president who lived in Eau Claire and was one of the founders of minor league ball in the city. Four days later, at 9:22 A.M. on June 18, 1952, the contract was stamped "approved." Henry Louis Aaron was officially a pro baseball player. Yet he knew he would be in the pros only as long as he was producing, especially if he read his contract carefully. Paragraph 5b said: "This contract may be terminated at any time by the Club or by any assignee by giving official release notice to the player."

Aaron officially replaced veteran outfielder Earl Bass on the Bears roster. Bass was a fan favorite, mostly because he hit a home run in the last game of the 1949 season to give the Bears the pennant. Bass, from North Carolina, had moved up to Class B ball at Jackson, Mississippi, in the Southern League in 1950 and Class A ball at Hartford, Connecticut, in the Eastern League in 1951. He was back in Class C in 1952 and hitting just .220 with the Bears before Aaron arrived. Bass still was bothered by a fractured ankle he had suffered a few seasons before. It wasn't the only time another player's broken ankle would figure in Aaron's advancement; in 1954, Bobby Thomson's broken ankle in spring training would open a spot for the rookie Aaron on the Milwaukee Braves' roster.

The struggling Bears also made other roster moves, including sending infielders Jim "Lucky" Fairchild and John Dobeck and pitcher Gene Derwinski down to Class D at Appleton in the Wisconsin State League. Fairchild's departure left the shortstop position open for Aaron. The first

CLASS C

Uniform Player Contract 1952 JUN 13 AM 9:22

APPROVED BY THE

NATIONAL ASSOCIATION

OF

PROFESSIONAL BASEBALL LEAGUES

IMPORTANT NOTICES

The attention of both Club and Player is specifically directed to the following excerpt from Rule 3 (a), of the Major-Minor League Rules:

"No Club shall make a contract different from the uniform contract and no club shall make a contract containing a non-reserve clause, except permission be first secured from the . . . President of the National Association. The making of any agreement between a Club and Player not embodied in the contract shall subject both parties to discipline."

A copy of this contract when executed must be delivered to player either in person or by registered mail, return receipt requested.

SALARY CERTIFICATE

This Contract will not be approved by the President of the National Association unless the Salary Certificate set forth below is executed by both the Club Official concerned and the Player.

_____ Walter J. Brock _____, the undersigned _____ Business Manager _____
Name of Club Official   Title

of the _____ Eau Claire _____ club, and _____ Henry Aaron _____
Name of Club   Name of Player

the player, each does hereby certify that all of the compensation player _____ Henry Aaron _____ is receiving or has been promised in the form of salary, transportation (except transportation expense for one person from the player's home on point of departure to the city to which he is directed to report), allowance in bonus whatever in nature from any club, person, agent, organization or corporation during the life of this Agreement or thereafter or has been paid prior to the execution of said contract, if incident to the signing thereof, by any club, person, agent, organization or corporation is set forth in the contract to which this certificate is attached.

We, and each of us execute this certificate with full knowledge that if its contents be found false, the club and the undersigned player may each be fined an amount not in excess of Five Hundred Dollars ($500.00) and the president and/or the undersigned official may be suspended from participation in National Association affairs and/or the undersigned player suspended, for a period of not to exceed two (2) years from the date the decision is rendered finding said certificate to be false, all as the President of the National Association may determine.

_____ Henry Aaron _____
PLAYER

_____ Walter J Brock _____
AUTHORIZED OFFICIAL OF CLUB

Henry Aaron earned $350 a month in 1952 from his first minor league contract with the Boston Braves and Eau Claire Bears. He did not receive a signing bonus.

(Courtesy of the National Baseball Hall of Fame)

month of the season had been a tough one on Fairchild, a twenty-three-year-old rookie from Long Island, New York. In his first game with the Bears, he made two errors. "It was awful. Too nervous, I guess," he surmised. He committed fifteen errors in his first fourteen games, which was a Northern League record. Fairchild attended a prep school as a teenager then went to Princeton University, helping the team win an Ivy League championship. All his education wasn't an advantage in Eau Claire; he was replaced by an inexperienced, immature shortstop who had dropped out of high school that spring to play pro baseball. Fairchild, like many people, had to wonder, "Who is Henry Aaron?"

That night, June 14, after he signed the contract, Aaron suited up for the first time when the Bears took on the first-place Rox, a farm team for the New York Giants, the team Aaron didn't sign with, the team that someday would realize it could have had Willie Mays and Henry Aaron in the same outfield. At game time, the temperature was eighty-six degrees and humid—Alabama weather. Aaron donned his Bears uniform for the first time, the word *Bears* in red script across the front of the white wool, button-up jersey and number 6 on the back. The baggy pants fell down

In 1952 Henry Aaron went from the Indianapolis Clowns of the Negro Leagues to the Eau Claire Bears of the Class C Northern League, where he played with and against white athletes for the first time.

(Photo courtesy of Shirley Reitmeier)

to about midcalf, where they were met with stirrup socks. Like all the players, he brought his own shoes and glove, the only parts of the uniform the club didn't provide. His still-developing postadolescent frame looked lean, almost underfed as if he had been away from his mother's cooking for several months, which he had. The Bears wore navy blue caps with red bills. The insignia was an oversized C encircling an E.

Players dressed in a spartan locker room that had wood slats over a dirt floor, which sometimes turned muddy after a rain. The Bears learned to get to the park early to claim one of the few nails on which to hang their gloves and clothes on the sloped ceiling, which was directly under the grandstand. After the game, they took turns showering in a musty two-nozzle stall. Yet they weren't complaining; until that season, visiting players didn't have any dressing room or a shower. The Bears were a privileged few taking part in pro baseball, the only sport that really mattered in the 1950s, except maybe boxing. Professional football, basketball, golf, tennis, and other sports made headlines but they weren't followed by the masses the way baseball was.

It was a 6 P.M. game, and 1,250 fans had paid one dollar for a box seat or seventy cents for general admission to see the Bears' latest Major League prospect. Kids in the Knot Hole Gang had paid thirty-five cents for the entire season. A box seat season ticket was only fifty-four dollars for 125 games, about the price of a good seat to one Major League game today. It was a simple time, monetarily. With another dollar in their pockets, fans could buy plenty to keep them busy between pitches: a scorecard, a seat cushion, peanuts, popcorn, a hot dog, a soda, and an ice cream—and still have a dime left over to call Lightning Cab if they needed a ride home.

Behind the plate that night was Emory "Ham" Olive, the umpire-in-chief for the Northern League and an Eau Claire resident. He knew what Aaron was going through by traveling with the Clowns and trying to succeed in pro ball, all on the road. After playing minor league ball in the 1920s in the International League in Newark, New Jersey, and Buffalo, New York, Olive became one of the nation's most popular baseball comics. In the 1930s and early 1940s, he played center field and managed the motley-looking House of David team throughout the West and western Canada. The House of David team represented a charismatic religious organization of the same name from Benton Harbor, Michigan. Emulating the accepted

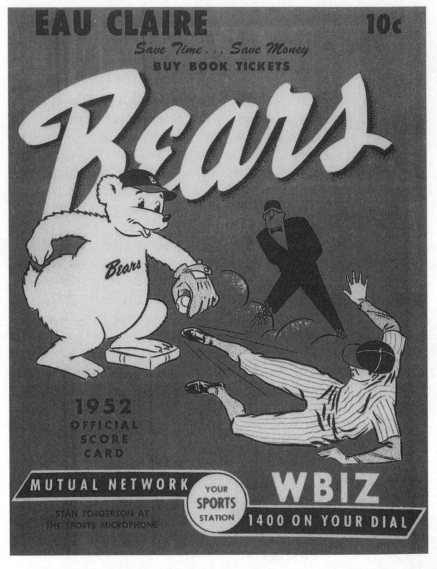

The Eau Claire Bears had high hopes for the 1952 season after winning
the Northern League championship in 1951.

image of Jesus Christ, the players all wore long hair and beards, but they didn't necessarily believe in the sect's apostolic tenets of eating no meat and donating all their worldly goods for the benefit of mankind. They simply were baseball emissaries. They were paid a minimum of $190 a month.

Olive claimed to have invented the game of pepper, a pregame shadow-ball drill that House of David was known for and a version of which became a staple among major leaguers. Some people would come just to see the House of David play pepper, then leave before the game began, Olive recalled. The House of David played up to ten exhibition games a week in big and small cities while traveling up to sixty thousand miles a year. They were a white version of the Indianapolis Clowns in the 1930s; there also was a black version of the House of David. The white House of David team played black teams like the New Orleans Crescent Stars and became famous for their tours with the Kansas City Monarchs, Jackie Robinson's old Negro League team.

Ham Olive was the umpire behind the plate on June 14, 1952, when Henry Aaron played his first game for the Eau Claire Bears.

(Photo courtesy of the *Eau Claire Leader-Telegram*)

On September 6, 1934, the House of David, also sometimes known as the Israelite House of David, played an exhibition night game in Eau Claire. It traveled with its own portable light plant, considered the largest in the world, for night games because most stadiums still were without lights. On the roster was a woman, Mildred Ella Didrikson, also known as "Babe," the world record hurdler and javelin thrower from the 1932 Olympics and soon-to-be champion golfer. Babe's role with House of David was to show up on time, pitch one inning, and leave. She didn't travel with the team but kept a schedule and drove her own car to the games. At the time, she also was playing on the Babe Didrikson's All-Americans, a women's basketball team, and earning about a thousand dollars a month with the two jobs during the Depression. She had long hair too, but Babe—nicknamed after Babe Ruth because of her athletic skills—was the one without the beard. A paragraph in the *Eau Claire Leader* the night before the game said, "Miss Didrikson will pitch at least a portion of the game and will ask no favors from her male opponents." Didrikson showed up with an infected finger and wasn't able to pitch, but she did appear as a pinch-hitter, drew a walk, and scored the House of David's only run in a 6–1 loss.

Fresh from the not-always-serious Clowns, Aaron walked onto Carson Park field for the first time and saw a half-filled stadium of curious white people staring at him from the covered wooden grandstand and metal auxiliary bleachers down the lines. "I was scared as hell," he said years later. Shy as he was, he probably kept his eyes off the crowd and on the field, a chain-link outfield fence, and a "Home of the Eau Claire Bears" scoreboard. In center field was a flagpole that carried the Bears' 1951 Northern League pennant, which had been hoisted two weeks earlier by Herman White, the league president and Eau Claire's city council president. Beyond left field was a football stadium; beyond center and right fields were softball fields, tennis courts, and Half Moon Lake.

Aaron had doubts, not necessarily about his ability but his situation. He had grown up with the impression that white people were superior in every way. How could he forget the sound and the feel of racism—his dinner plate being smashed at a Washington, D.C., restaurant only weeks earlier with the Clowns because he, a black man, had eaten off it? How could he not recall that just months earlier white people in his hometown wouldn't dare be seen with him, not in school, in church, on a bus, at a restaurant, at a drinking fountain, and certainly not on a baseball field?

He had never faced a white pitcher in his life. Were they faster than black pitchers? Were their curve balls better? Did they know something he didn't? Would he be able to hit a white man? Were they really a superior race?

Just the prospect of facing that fear, all alone in a city far from home at age eighteen, might have been enough to send many people to the Union bus depot. Mobile had to look pretty inviting to Aaron that night. Homesickness ruined many a promising baseball career. For example, in 1951 the Chicago White Sox gave a $15,000 bonus to third baseman Luis Garcia of Venezuela. Garcia had played for the Aberdeen Pheasants, in the Northern League. But Garcia became homesick, gave the money back, and went home. Alas, Garcia was back with the Pheasants in 1952. Aaron faced loneliness as well as a great cultural divide when he walked on the field for the first time in Eau Claire. He was comforted only in knowing that Jackie Robinson, Larry Doby, Willie Mays, and other blacks had passed the white test. Would he?

Aaron didn't come to bat in the first inning, although he started in the field at shortstop. Aaron batted seventh in player-manager Marion "Bill" Adair's lineup. Leading off was first baseman Dick Engquist followed by second baseman Pat Patterson, left fielder Wes Covington, catcher "Julie" Bowers, right fielder Lantz Blaney, center fielder Chester Morgan, the ex-Clown Aaron, third baseman Ron Gendreau, and pitcher Bobby Brown. Adair and Bill Conroy also saw action in the game as substitutes. Among the pitchers was Don Jordan, a hometown product and fan favorite who had a 16-6 record the previous pennant year. Pitchers Jordan, Brown, and Gordon Roach along with Morgan were holdovers from the 1951 pennant team.

In the second inning, trailing 2–0, the Bears began a rally when Morgan doubled to the fence in right-center field. Aaron came to bat against Art Rosser of Saint Cloud and calmly cracked a clean, line drive single over third baseman Wray Upper to drive in Morgan, who had just come off the disabled list after twenty days with a blood clot in his leg. Aaron—either trying to make an impression or trying to emulate Jackie Robinson—tried to stretch the hit into a double but was thrown out.

In the fifth inning it was the same combination. Morgan doubled and Aaron singled in his second at bat—again a line drive to left—to drive in Morgan.

All the waiting was over for Aaron. He had his answer. "Hank Aaron, 18-year-old Negro shortstop, made an auspicious beginning by banging out singles in his first two trips," Buzzell wrote in the *Leader* the next day. Buzzell, like most media people at the time, often on first reference mentioned the race or nationality of players if they weren't white or American.

If Aaron's two line drive hits were harbingers of his Major League career, so was his play at shortstop. Aaron had a solid night fielding until he muffed a double-play ball in the sixth inning that gave the Rox the winning run. By the time he reached the majors in 1954, Aaron was an outfielder. Yet no one was blaming that night's 4–3 loss on Aaron. Several other players made rookie-type errors, and Covington went 0-for-5, striking out three times, once with the bases loaded and once in the bottom of the ninth with the tying run on second base as he looked at a called third strike.

Aaron's bat had to be a welcome sight to Bears fans, whose teams had won two of the last three Northern League pennants. In 1951 the Bears won the pennant by twelve games under Adair. He was back as manager, but his 1952 Bears were 17-20 and already thirteen games out of first place.

Only two days before Aaron arrived, Buzzell wrote an editorial about the team's sagging attendance the first month. Attendance was six thousand behind the 1951 figure for that date, and the team was beginning to worry about paying the bills. "Unless there is a big climb in attendance that holds up all season, there may be no Eau Claire Bears in 1953," Buzzell wrote. Although the weather had been poor in May, team officials and Buzzell surmised that low attendance figures could be blamed in part on the team's poor start, people listening to the radio broadcasts of the games, and others simply staying home to enjoy television, the latest form of entertainment.

Buzzell also mentioned a more volatile issue that may have been affecting attendance: "There have also been grumblings about the number of Negro players." The Bears started the season with four black players, their most ever. They were Covington, Bowers, pitcher Walt James of Puerto Rico and the Virgin Islands, and outfielder Orlando Casellas of Puerto

Rico. But two weeks into the season Casellas was sent to Class D Danville, Illinois, in the Mississippi–Ohio Valley League. Another two weeks later, James followed. Buzzell most likely raised the issue in his story because he had heard city residents—and maybe some club officials—complain. Even if he didn't give credence to the theory, he probably felt it was his responsibility to report what he had been hearing.

Were James and Casellas sent down because the Bears suddenly developed a black quota when early-season attendance was down? In the late 1940s and early 1950s, when pro baseball, football, and basketball were being integrated, many athletes felt they were victims of teams that set limits on how many black players could be on the roster. Teams often had an even number of blacks—often two—so that they could room together on the road. The arrangement wasn't necessarily for the black players; teams were heading off any potential complaints from white players who didn't want to sleep in the same room. Aaron's arrival boosted the number of black Bears to three, where it stayed the rest of the season. All three of them stayed at the YMCA; white players were offered rooms in private homes or in hotels. Only one white Bears player, pitcher Elmer Toth, stayed at the YMCA, but he doesn't remember associating with the three black players there. Thus, the white and black Bears players were segregated, but since Eau Claire had a YMCA but no black families, separate housing probably was the path of least resistance. Aaron didn't mind the arrangement and didn't make an issue of it. "It was fine with me," he said.

The Bears left spring training in Myrtle Beach, South Carolina, in late April with four black players, so when Aaron arrived in mid-June, his color wasn't a new issue with team members. He was just another young prospect trying to make the team. Pitcher Don Jordan recalled experiencing culture shock during spring training in the South when the Bears' black players were called names. "It was kind of a traumatic experience for me, a white boy from Eau Claire. I remember we drove up from spring training in Myrtle Beach and played an exhibition game at Bluefield, West Virginia, and we had to go into the restaurants and get the food for the black players. We'd get hamburgers and take them out for them to eat in the car. They couldn't eat in the restaurants with us."

The arrival of Aaron had to please Bears officials and fans. Within a week of Aaron's presence in the lineup, the Bears won 5 of 7 games, were 22-22, and were beginning to gain ground on Saint Cloud and Superior. After five home games, Aaron was batting .354. The team had made other changes that would make them more competitive, and Aaron was living up to his billing.

People began to talk about the Bears' new shortstop. Bill Anderson recalls being a fifteen-year-old team volunteer and getting admitted to games free. That wasn't the best part, though; he occasionally shagged balls, set up and took down box seats, chased balls in the bull pens, and drove a scooter with a sidecar to drag the infield with a screen before the game and in the middle of the fifth inning. "Everybody thought we were the luckiest guys in town," Anderson said. Sometimes Anderson would play catch with the players or try to get near them during warm-ups to see what they were like. The first time he saw Aaron up close, he couldn't believe the size of his wrists. "They were as big as my biceps. That was a topic of conversation for a couple of weeks with my friends. 'Did you see his wrists?' There was a sense of anticipation when he was up. He hit stingers. You just knew he was going to make it [to the big leagues]. And he had a good smile, you know."

Anderson may not have been exaggerating about Aaron's wrists. In an article in the *New York Times Magazine* of September 21, 1958, writer William Barry Furlong said Aaron's wrists "measure almost eight inches around, about one and a half to two inches more than the wrists of heavyweight [boxing] champion Floyd Patterson."

As Lloyd Berkvam and his nine-year-old son, Michael, were driving to the game against Saint Cloud on June 14, they listened to the pregame show on Eau Claire's station WBIZ. Announcer Stan Torgerson commented on the air how the new Bears shortstop looked young enough to be in junior high. "He looked just like a kid out of the sandlot," recalls Berkvam. "My impression was that I didn't think he was going to be a home run hitter." Despite the draining heat of the day, young Michael wore his Eau Claire Bears jacket, which got him into all games free.

Sitting on the third-base side at Aaron's first game was Howie Bullock, a catcher on the 1942 Bears team, which won the Northern League pennant. "The first ball hit to [Aaron] at shortstop he picked it up and threw it underhanded over to first. We said, 'What the hell was that?'" Bullock remembers. "But he got it there. He was something different. He seemed like he hit the ball right out of the catcher's glove. You'd think the ball was by him, then he'd snap those wrists and away it went. He didn't have a big, long swing. It was a lot of wrists and arms. They say when he was a kid he used to walk along the railroad tracks and hit bottle caps with a stick. You know how those caps flutter when they fall? That's probably how he developed those strong wrists."

Marty Crowe, a high school basketball coach and avid Bears fan at the time, thought Aaron was a special talent. "It must have been quite a thrill to be Hank Aaron back in 1952 because everyone knew that, if anybody, he was the one who would make it. Aaron was bound to catch the eye of the scouts because there aren't that many great natural hitters who come around, and he was a great natural hitter."

That was also the opinion of Billy Southworth, a scout for the Braves. He saw Aaron play two games in Eau Claire and was sold on him. "For a baby face kid of eighteen years, his playing ability is outstanding," he wrote to John Quinn, general manager of the Boston Braves. "He has good hands, also quick hands, gets the ball away fast and accurately. I saw him go deep in the hole to his right and field a slow hit ball. He came up throwing and virtually shot his man out going to first. This was a big league play in my book because I did not think he had a chance to retire the man at first. He has proven his ability in the short time he has been here. Aaron has all the qualifications of a Major League short-stop." He made little comment about Aaron's hitting other than his .345 average at the time. "He is a line drive hitter, although he has hit a couple of balls out of the park." Southworth was planning to see Aaron play two more games, but he sent his report early because "regardless of what happens tonight, it will not change my mind in the least about this boy's ability."

Southworth knew what he was talking about. An outfielder, he had played thirteen years in the majors, hitting .297 for a career that ended in 1929. His career highlight came in the 1926 World Series when he helped the Saint Louis Cardinals defeat the New York Yankees and Babe Ruth in seven games. Southworth batted .345 for the series with ten hits (more than future Hall of Famers Rogers Hornsby of Saint Louis or Babe Ruth and Lou Gehrig). Southworth then managed for thirteen years. In 1942 and 1944 he directed Saint Louis to World Series titles with a young Stan Musial in the lineup. In 1948 he managed the Boston Braves to a pennant with a young Warren Spahn on the pitching staff. In 1952 when he came to Eau Claire to see Aaron, Southworth was in his first year as a Braves scout after being let go as manager. He had played with and against and managed some of the game's greatest players. The Braves brass took Southworth seriously; they knew they had a winner down on the farm.

But Aaron didn't awe everyone, including some teammates. Bears pitcher Ken Reitmeier said, "You hear a lot of stories, people saying, 'I could tell right away he had Major League All-Star written all over him,' but it wasn't apparent on the field when he first came. On the field he did things wrong. He had a good swing, but he hit off the front foot, something you're never supposed to do. He played shortstop and threw underarm, something you're not supposed to do."

Harold "Diz" Kronenberg of Eau Claire had spent five years in the minor leagues. He saw Aaron play one game and was convinced. "I said he had a lot of talent but he'd never make it in the big leagues," said Kronenberg, who like many people didn't like Aaron's sidearm throwing style.

BLACK AND WHITE

Aaron was full of self-confidence on the field but not off it. He felt lonely and out of place at first in Eau Claire. A little girl at a restaurant stared at him so long she forgot to eat. He left the stadium one time and noticed a white man leaning against a car, his eyes riveted on Aaron. "It was an adjustment on everybody's part. They weren't used to seeing black people around, and I wasn't used to being around white people. It was something a lot of black players went through in the minor leagues back then. You can't imagine how alone we felt," Aaron wrote in his autobiography, *I Had a Hammer*.

He wasn't the first black player in Eau Claire. Billy Bruton and Roy White broke the color barrier in 1950, three years after Jackie Robinson did the same in the Major Leagues at Brooklyn. The Boston Braves integrated their Major League team at the same time as their minor league Eau Claire Bears; Sam Jethroe became the first black player in a Braves uniform on April 18, 1950. In 1949 the color barrier was broken a hundred miles away from Eau Claire in Minneapolis when Negro League great Ray Dandridge and another player joined the Minneapolis Millers of the American Association.

The prospect of having black players was of great concern to the Bears management because they didn't know how the fans would react. One day in the early spring of 1950, club president Randall Bezanson was walking downtown with his son when a fan angrily warned him that bringing blacks to the city would cause ticket sales to dive. In early April 1950, Bezanson sent a letter to manager Andy Cohen at spring training explaining that the issue was potentially divisive. One high-ranking Bears official told Cohen to try not to return with any black players. On April 14, 1950, Cohen replied. "Didn't realize the reaction would be quite so stirring. We'll try to select the best baseball club possible and hope it will satisfy the fans.... Make up your mind. The Negro player is here to stay. I predict the time is not too far off when he will be playing in the South. Brother Rickey is the great Emancipator," wrote Cohen, who played from 1926 to 1929 with the New York Giants. "Brother Rickey" was a reference to Dodgers president Branch Rickey, who signed Jackie Robinson.

On March 30, three weeks before Bruton and White were named to the Bears roster, the *Leader* carried a four-paragraph story that the local Toastmasters club had voted against black ballplayers. "Eau Claire is not a suitable city for a Negro baseball player, a majority of the members of the Toastmasters club decided Tuesday night," the story began. The sports pages had been carrying rumors, and the issue was being discussed in offices, barbershops, and bars and around dinner tables. Some of the Toastmasters, a group of business leaders, thought that bringing blacks to the city to play baseball was the same as inviting trouble. They cited housing problems, the lack of other blacks to associate with, and possible poor treatment by city fans. They probably thought that Bruton, from Philadelphia, might face the same treatment in Eau Claire as world renowned opera singer Marian Anderson, "The Lady from Philadelphia." Shortly before Bruton arrived, Anderson had been denied a room at the Hotel Eau Claire because she was black.

The Toastmasters story ignited a heated debate among city residents. In the next few weeks, fourteen letters to the editor were published on the opinion page. Since relatively few people ever write letters to the newspaper, those fourteen likely represented the concerns of many thousands of readers. The majority of the letter writers, eleven, favored black players while publicly shaming the Toastmasters as intolerant, hypocritical, and un-American. The other three letters cited old arguments about blacks and whites not belonging on the same side of the tracks. "We feel that the community has been disgraced by this action of the Toastmasters club," wrote Mae Fancher of the First Congregational Church. "What would it be like if God would lock the pearly gate because a man was not the right color," wrote Joseph Johnson. One anonymous writer said the Toastermasters should be branded "as down right STINKERS."

The black players also got a vote of confidence from one city church and Local 119 of the Rubber Workers Union at the tire factory. "There should not be a question of any city in these United States as not being suitable for a player of any race, creed or color," a union statement said. The president of the union remarked, "If Eau Claire is not a suitable city for a Negro baseball player ... then Eau Claire had better get back into the United States."

As 1950 spring training wore on in Myrtle Beach it became apparent that the speedy Bruton, described in the *Leader* as a "fleet colored boy," would make the team. A year earlier, he was discovered playing for the semipro San Francisco Cubs, a black team that traveled the Northern Plains and Canada. Bruton's speed caught the eye of Cohen. "Bruton is the fastest man in camp and has proven it by winning every race held," Cohen reported. On April 22 the *Leader* reported that Bruton had signed an Eau Claire contract.

A native of Panola, Alabama, near Birmingham, Bruton was twenty-four years old but said he was twenty so that scouts would give him a chance. He had wanted to be a chemist, but "I took the [baseball] offer because I knew it would be hard for a Negro to get a good job as a chemist." He was headed north for the summer with Roy White, a 138-pound pitcher from Austin, Texas.

The race issue fizzled in Eau Claire, although the *Leader* of April 27 didn't help matters by running a photo of Eau Claire's first two black players and, elsewhere in the paper, a photo of three white elementary students performing in blackface at a local minstrel show. Some of the Toastmasters must have been secretly smiling. The picture of Bruton and White— put in only so that people could stare at their skin color—was bad enough. It was just the two of them, both down on their right knees, their left arms dangling nonchalantly over their left legs, White holding his glove and Bruton his bat. The caption read: "First Colored Bears. Roy White and Bill Bruton, the first two colored players ever to perform for the Eau Claire

Bears, are pictured above at the Myrtle Beach, S.C., training camp. White, a pitcher with plenty of speed, hails from Austin, Texas, and Bruton, an outfielder and fastest player in the camp, is from Philadelphia."

Bruton and White became popular with the fans. Bruton, who rented a room from high school basketball coach Marty Crowe, set a league record with sixty-six stolen bases and was 1950 Northern League Rookie of the Year. "Ninety-nine percent of the people in Eau Claire welcomed us wholeheartedly," Bruton said, which was far more than he could say about the way he was treated in the still-segregated South during Braves spring training in subsequent years. "I enjoyed it that year. I just tried to go out and play my best, to turn the jeers into cheers." Carl "Red" Wyczawski, the sports reporter who covered Bruton's arrival, was the official scorer for Bruton's first game. He recalled that when Bruton was introduced at Carson Park, "He got a wonderful ovation from the fans."

Billy Bruton was one of two players who broke the color barrier in Eau Claire with the 1950 Bears, three years after Jackie Robinson was the first black player in the major leagues. He later played in the same outfield with Henry Aaron in Milwaukee.

(Photo courtesy of the *Eau Claire Leader-Telegram*)

White, who had a good curve ball but was not an outstanding pitcher, didn't last long with the Bears. He also started dating a white woman in Eau Claire in 1950, but Wyczawski doesn't know if that led to White's departure. "You had to be careful," Wyczawski said.

Bruton eventually became one of the most popular Milwaukee Braves. As a rookie, he scored the first run in the 1953 season opener after they had relocated from Boston. And a few days later in the first game ever played at Milwaukee County Stadium, he homered in the bottom of the tenth inning—off the glove of Enos Slaughter in right field—to give the new Milwaukee Braves a 3–2 victory over the Saint Louis Cardinals. He was hailed as the fastest man in the majors. The "Ebony Comet" won three straight National League stolen base titles and helped the Braves win two pennants and a World Series. Wyczawski went to work for the public relations department for the Braves from 1954 to 1956, was the public address announcer at County Stadium, and became a close friend of Bruton's. He called Bruton "a prince of a guy, the best kind to break the color barrier. He was one of the greatest guys I ever knew." But the racism Bruton encountered took its toll. Bruton once confided to Wyczawski: "Red, there are times I'd give my left arm to be white."

Bruton also played in Major League Baseball's first all-black outfield, also known as the "ABC outfield." In 1957 the Braves had Aaron in right, Bruton in center, and Wes Covington in left. All three had played their first seasons in that city up north, Eau Claire. Bruton died in 1995 at age sixty-nine near his home in Wilmington, Delaware.

Another black player for the 1951 Bears was the multitalented Horace Garner. He was considered a terrific all-around athlete. One coach called the six-feet-six, 230-pound Garner "the team." His arm was legendary; he could stand at home plate and *throw* balls over the center field fence. Maybe that ability came from his unusually long arms, so long in fact that he once reached down to his shoe tops to catch a fly ball in the outfield and stepped on his nonglove hand, spiking himself in the process. He also could hit—he led the league in hitting in 1951 at .359 and was Northern League Rookie of the Year. He was the top hitter despite being hit by pitches seventeen times. In those days, the brushback pitch was part of every hurler's arsenal, and it was especially threatening because players still wore only cloth caps, not helmets, to the plate. As a black man who led the league in hitting, Garner had to know that his head, his ribs, and his back were the targets for many frustrated pitchers. He didn't back down. He hit in Eau Claire, Evansville, Indiana, and in 1953 in Jacksonville, Florida, as Aaron's Southern Atlantic (Sally) League teammate. Yet something went wrong, and Garner never made the majors. Many years later, he was seen hauling garbage in Ames, Iowa.

Aaron said he was thankful for Bruton paving the way. In Jacksonville in 1953 Aaron found out what it was like to break a color barrier when he, Garner, and several opposing players integrated the Sally League and endured a season of racial slurs and taunts. "Bruton certainly made things a lot easier for the rest of us in Eau Claire. By the end of his season there, he was the most popular player on the team—and that was no small thing in a town where women and girls were warned not to walk down the street with him," Aaron wrote in *I Had a Hammer*. A chef in Eau Claire once refused to cook a steak for Bruton because he was black. In 1952 one of the local restaurants offered a steak dinner to any Bear who hit a home run. When the Bears hitting the most home runs turned out to be black— Aaron, Covington, and Bowers—the regulars at the restaurant complained about the mixed company. The promotion abruptly was canceled.

Aaron, Bowers, and Covington were the three black players who played the majority of the season with the Bears. William Julius "Julie" Bowers from Staten Island, New York, was five-feet-ten, 175 pounds, and the oldest—twenty-three. Bowers was a rookie, but he had played semipro ball with the Black Yankee Travelers and saw action in thirty games with Hartford in 1951 in the Class A Eastern League. He started strong in Eau Claire, hitting over .400 the first month, committing only one error, and catching every game. Clell Buzzell even wrote a feature story on Bowers, accompanied by a photo. Maybe some fans didn't like the idea of four blacks starting the season with the Bears, but Buzzell was making it clear that Bowers, for one, belonged there.

John Wesley "Wes" Covington, age twenty, was a six-feet-one, 205-pound rookie from Laurinburg, North Carolina. He earned the nickname "Flash" for his 9.9-second speed in the hundred-yard dash. He was an all-state fullback and a track star in high school, but he chose baseball and signed with the Braves. Although he led the Bears with twenty-four homers and ninety-nine runs batted in and hit .330 in 1952, his career was sidetracked when he served in the army in 1953 and 1954. In 1955, after he was discharged, he followed in Aaron's footsteps by hitting .326 to lead the Sally League (Aaron had led the league in 1953).

Covington made the majors as Aaron's teammate the very next season with the Milwaukee Braves. He played eleven seasons in the majors with six teams, retiring in 1966. Covington had a .279 career batting average and 131 home runs, fifty-five of them with the Braves in 1957 and 1958. He made game-saving catches in two 1957 World Series games when the Braves won the crown, but he was considered an average fielder and was bothered by injuries much of his career. Covington took a job as an advertising consultant with the *Edmonton Sun* newspaper in Canada, where he was still working in 2000.

In 1952 Covington was hit in the head by a pitched ball and spent two weeks at Luther Hospital across Half Moon Lake. The injury turned into an experience in race relations he never forgot. As he described it in Aaron's *I Had a Hammer*:

Julius "Julie" Bowers played catcher for the Eau Claire Bears in 1952 and roomed at the YMCA with Henry Aaron and Wes Covington.

(Photo courtesy of Shirley Reitmeier)

I was the first black person who ever went into the hospital there. I felt like a sideshow freak. They assigned different nurses to me every day so they could all get the experience of being in my presence. Actually, I was treated very nicely. The nurses would open my mail and water the flowers for me. All but this one. One nurse, a lady who must have been sixty or seventy years old, had the job of putting water in my pitcher every day. This pitcher was on a tray by the door, and I'd look up and see this arm coming around the door and picking up the pitcher. Then the arm would come around and put the pitcher back. I never saw anything more than the arm. Then one day I was out of bed when she came, and I looked at her. She just froze. I said something, and she just stared at me. She poured the water very nervously, then left. I asked somebody about it later, and they said she had just never seen a black person before and didn't know what to expect. Well, one day I was close enough to the door and I handed her the pitcher. Then she started to acknowledge me, like bowing her head real fast. Finally, she said something. After that, we had a little conversation, and by the time I left the hospital, she was sitting at the side of the bed talking to me like an old friend.

Even though black players preceded him in Eau Claire and he had two black teammates, life still wasn't easy for Aaron in Eau Claire. He was naturally reserved, and he was cautious about speaking his mind after growing up in a city that legally silenced his feelings. "I wasn't much of a talker anyway, but in Eau Claire you couldn't pry my mouth open. It didn't take much to tell that my way of talking was different than the way people talked in Wisconsin, and I felt freakish enough as it was," Aaron said in *I Had a Hammer*. Clayton Anderson, the manager at the YMCA, played basketball with Aaron on rainy days but couldn't get him to talk. "He was very shy and lonesome. He didn't talk about it, but you could tell," Anderson said. Ron Buckli, a sixteen-year-old budding athlete who hung out at the YMCA, played dice with Aaron and saw firsthand his anxiety. Aaron would "walk from one corner of the building to the other, cautiously checking each street. Then he would return quickly and roll the dice." Buckli went on to play in the minor leagues himself, became the local sports editor, and wrote stories about Aaron for the next fifty years.

Aaron's best friends were Bowers and Covington, but the outgoing Covington would tease Aaron, straining their relationship. "Even I had to gain his trust. He just would not open up to you," Covington said in a 1993 interview with the *Leader-Telegram*. "Hank was as far away from me at times as he was from anybody else on the ball club. He was a very private individual. I don't think at that time we were really trying to be close. We were just trying so damn hard to make the team." Aaron, Covington, and Bowers occasionally went into Smitty's 202 Club two blocks from the Y. One woman in Eau Claire said she recalled seeing Aaron in one booth and Covington and Bowers in another.

One incident at the YMCA showed just how sensitive Aaron was. Diz Kronenberg, the former minor league player who worked the night shift at the Y, often was at work when Aaron, Bowers, and Covington returned from games. "The four of us would sit there and talk baseball, but Aaron never spoke. He'd go sit on the windowsill, but Covington would razz him and get his dander up a little bit. One time Covington razzed Aaron about his hitting and wouldn't let up. Aaron pulled a jacknife out of his pocket and put it up over his head. He was perturbed. Wes just laughed at him. Nothing happened. It was just one of those things," Kronenberg said.

John "Wes" Covington was a power-hitting rookie outfielder for the Eau Claire Bears in 1952 and one of Henry Aaron's friends. Covington later played in the Milwaukee Braves outfield with Aaron.

(Photo courtesy of Shirley Reitmeier)

THE START OF ONE CAREER,
THE END OF ANOTHER

Aaron's .354 batting average the first week was as good as he could hope for, but his second week was about as bad as possible. On June 20, one week after making his debut, the Bears played the Superior Blues at Carson Park. Aaron fielded a ball at shortstop, stepped on the bag at second, and fired to first in a double-play attempt. But the ball hit Superior catcher Chuck Wiles as he slid into second base.

Wiles was about one foot from the ball when it came off Aaron's hand. Aaron's sidearm or underarm style of throwing, releasing the ball below his hips instead of over his head, may have put the ball directly in line with Wiles's head. Eau Claire pitcher Don Jordan vividly remembers the play, however, and said Wiles could have avoided the injury by sliding earlier or getting out of the base path to the right. Players did not wear batting helmets in the early 1950s. Some wore plastic inserts around the rim of the cap to protect their temporal lobes, but their ears still were uncovered. Aaron's throw hit Wiles squarely on his right ear, and the sound echoed all the way to the dugouts. "Boy did he catch it," Bears pitcher Ken Reitmeier said, remembering the sickening sound. Wiles went down, briefly regained consciousness, and was taken by ambulance across Half Moon Lake to Luther Hospital for observation. At the hospital, Wiles lapsed into a coma for three days. When Wiles's wife, Alice, arrived at the hospital, she took one look at her unconscious, bruised, swollen husband, fell to her knees, and began to pray. She had been listening to the game on the radio in Superior but had no idea how severe the injury was. Doctors said that if the impact of the ball hadn't been cushioned by the outer ear, Wiles would have been killed instantly.

The loss of Wiles cost the Blues the game, not that they cared much. Substitute pitcher Alfredo Ibanez, a twenty-two-year-old rookie from Cuba, replaced Wiles as catcher. Ibanez let two pitches get past him, allowing the tying and go-ahead runs to score as the Bears won 5–4 and swept the three-game series.

After two weeks at the hospital, Wiles was released but his life had changed forever. Aaron's throw destroyed Wiles's inner ear, altering his equilibrium and sense of balance. He spent months learning to walk again. For several years he suffered from severe concussion headaches. Two years

after the accident, he had the inner ear removed in an operation at Mayo
Clinic in Rochester, Minnesota. Doctors told Wiles that he wouldn't work
the rest of his life because of his disability.

Wiles had played as high as Class A ball with the White Sox organization but agreed to go to Class C Superior in 1952 as a favor to the White
Sox. In return, he received double pay and a guarantee to go to spring
training with the Major League White Sox the next season. That dream
was over. Wiles, his wife, and their young son went home to Albemarle,
North Carolina, where Chuck decided to give baseball one more try. In
1953 he joined the Cotton Mill Boys, a local semipro team, and began
playing. "One time I got to second base. I was determined I was going to
get home." He tried to score on a hit, but he became so disoriented rounding the bases that he couldn't find home plate. "I don't think I even knew
where I was. I missed home plate by a lot. The fans thought I was clowning," Wiles said. That night, Alice made Chuck promise that he never
would play baseball again. And he didn't.

With his career over, he and Alice moved to Seville, Florida, where Alice
supported the family by working in customer service at Sears for thirty-
four years. Chuck took up fly rod fishing for largemouth bass (he once
held three world records), kept a positive attitude, and became thankful
despite continuing health problems, including several small strokes most
likely related to his head injury. At times he has difficulty hearing and
speaking. "The injury made us appreciate every day, every day," Alice
Wiles said. "I feel very fortunate to be alive. I really do," Chuck Wiles
said. He holds no grudge against Aaron but seems puzzled why he has
never made an attempt to apologize in person.

Does Wiles ever wonder what his life would have been like without the
injury? "You better believe it," he said. He told a story of going to the mall
where Alice worked in Daytona Beach, Florida, and striking up a conversation with a man who turned out to be from Superior. Wiles quizzed
him about the 1952 Blues, and to his amazement the man knew the entire
lineup. "I asked him who the catcher was. He said, 'Chuck Wiles. The
best damn catcher the Blues ever had, but Hank Aaron hit him on the
head and killed him.'" Wiles turned to the man and said to his surprise,
"You've got everything right but the last part. I'm Chuck Wiles."

Wiles was having a good season, hitting .309, with the Blues when his
career ended.

On July 16, 1952, at the Northern League All-Star Game in Superior, Wiles needed help walking. In fact, young outfielder Len Vandehey of Sioux Falls said years later that he remembered only one thing about that game—the sad sight of Wiles being guided into the room where the stars had gathered for a banquet. At the game, the overflow crowd of 5,318 fans passed the hat and raised $723 to help Wiles.

Ironically, it was Wiles who may have prevented Aaron from getting hit on the head in 1952. When a brushback pitch came Aaron's way in that series, Wiles, as was his custom with all players, remembers that he told Aaron to be prepared. Aaron used to see more brushback pitches than most players, Wiles said, "because we couldn't get him out."

The errant throw ended Wiles's career and almost ended Aaron's. He was upset at himself for hurting Wiles. Aaron was still eighteen and away from home for the first time. After three months of loneliness and now heartache, Aaron was more discouraged than ever, even though he was succeeding on the field. The Superior fans had started booing Aaron and kept it up the rest of the season. "I really and truly felt sorry for him because the Superior fans were on him bad, really bad," Wiles said of Aaron. He called home from the YMCA one night and said he was quitting, coming back to Mobile. "My brother, Herbert Junior, took the phone and told me I'd be crazy to leave. He said there was nothing to come home to, and if I left I'd be walking out on the best break I could ever hope to get. Years later, when I talked with other black players, I found out that a lot of them almost quit the minor leagues. Billy Williams actually left his team in Amarillo, Texas, and went back home to Mobile. But when he got there, all his friends and kids from the neighborhood kept swarming around him and asking about pro ball, and he realized he was about to blow a chance that the rest of them dreamed about—which was exactly what Herbert Junior said to me," Aaron recalled in *I Had a Hammer*.

Aaron struck up a friendship with two of Wiles's teammates, six-feet-four Bob Bennett and six-feet-six Dan Phalen. Phalen was the Northern League Most Valuable Player in 1951. The Superior Blues stayed at the posh Hotel Eau Claire, and several times Aaron met his friendly rivals for breakfast in the coffee shop a block from the YMCA. In the 185-seat Colonial Grill, where fresh flowers were always on the table, waiters dressed in white vests and shirts with dark ties, and waitresses wore dark button-up dresses and white waist aprons, Aaron confessed his fears to the two white men. "He was more depressed than he indicated. It was a serious thing. He wanted to quit," Bennett said. "He expressed the feeling that 'If I'm going to kill somebody in baseball, I'm not going to play baseball.' He'd talk a lot about loneliness, homesickness, that there were no black girls in Eau Claire."

Bennett, twenty-two, knew about homesickness. Like most of the other single players for the Blues, he was living at the YMCA in Superior. He also was used to helping displaced ballplayers. A native of Cicero, Illinois, he had played in the Mexican League and now was the interpreter for two players from Havana, Cuba, José Bustamentes and Alfredo Ibanez, who were playing for the Blues and knew almost no English. Bennett could see through Aaron's sadness and loneliness and recognize a good person and talented athlete. "We kept telling him to hang on because you'll go someplace. Stardom was written all over him. He was nice to talk to, just a nice kid, and what a great athlete."

Bennett was a good example of perseverance for Aaron. In 1950 Bennett was hit in the head by a pitch that fractured his skull. On Memorial Day in 1952, he was hit by a pitch that broke his jaw and left him unconscious for nearly two days. But he came back and helped the Blues win the Northern League title. And he never stopped helping people. When his baseball career ended, he became a police officer in Superior and eventually became chief of police.

Aaron never spoke to Wiles after the accident. Wiles believed that Aaron—as young as he was—couldn't bring himself to apologize or didn't know how to apologize in person. Later on, in books and in a television documentary about his life, Aaron always expressed regret about hitting Wiles. The messages got through to Wiles, although not as loud and clear as if they had been delivered in person.

The incident haunted Aaron for years. In 1956, *Saturday Evening Post* writer Furman Bisher said one of the reasons Aaron didn't play shortstop or second base in the majors is that he "candidly admitted he did not like the idea of having base runners bearing down on him in the middle of double plays."

THE TALK OF THE TOWN

On June 22 Aaron boosted his morale when he hit his first home run in organized baseball. It came in an 8–4 win over Fargo-Moorhead in Fargo.

To Aaron, the homer probably wasn't significant because he had hit several with the Clowns, his first pro team. Yet back then the term *organized baseball* meant every professional team except the ones in the Negro Leagues. If white ball was organized ball, black ball had to be the opposite, or so Americans were led to believe by the white businessmen and the media who spoke of organized ball. The implication was that blacks couldn't organize a baseball league the way whites could. But if the Negro Leagues had schedules, umpires, salaries, paid admission, a World Series, and so forth, why wasn't it considered organized baseball? Maybe the slight involved the same arrogance that led baseball officials to call its championship the World Series when it was—and still is—the championship of just one nation. Pro baseball owners have always been a secret fraternity with one goal, ensuring their profitability through sometimes unscrupulous business decisions.

At the time of Aaron's first homer in Fargo, a hometown boy named Roger Maris was a few months shy of eighteen years old. That spring, while Aaron was with the Clowns, Maris was still in high school, winning the 100-yard dash, 200-yard dash, and shot put in the Fargo all-city track meet. He was flashing that combination of speed and power that someday would make him a home run hitter for the New York Yankees, an athlete so good that he would break Babe Ruth's single-season home run record. In 1952 Maris played for a Fargo-Moorhead amateur baseball team that played on the same field as the Northern League teams. In 1953 Maris followed Aaron's path to the Northern League, where he would play for Fargo-Moorhead.

Aaron's first home run came off Reuben Stohs, a veteran left-handed pitcher. Stohs never made the Major Leagues and retired in Seward, Nebraska, after thirty years as a minister, teacher, and coach. He spent six seasons in the minor leagues, along the way playing with famous Yankees pitchers Ryne Duren and Don Larsen. But Stohs is most famous for giving up Aaron's first home run. "I live in ignominy," he said. When he saw Aaron for the first time at old Barnett Field in Fargo, he couldn't figure out why a Fargo-Moorhead official had said Aaron was going to be great. "We all tried to figure out how this skinny kid playing shortstop was a fantastic talent. The only way we could figure out was picking up ground balls." Aaron didn't look like much of a hitter to Stohs until Stohs threw a pitch high in the strike zone, about cap high, and Aaron "got up on his tiptoes and hit it out. What made Aaron so great was the quickness of his wrists, the quickness of his bat." Years later Stohs saw Aaron and Maris at spring training—the two teenagers with ties to Fargo—and got their autographs on a baseball. He once had developed a personality test that was used by many Major League teams. He had to wonder what traits they had in common that helped them break Babe Ruth's records.

After a few weeks, Aaron was the talk of Eau Claire and the Northern League. He was leading the league in hitting with a sizzling .386 average. After just twenty-six games, he had twenty runs batted in and had fourteen games with two or more hits. He was igniting the Bears, who won ten straight games in late June and nineteen of their first twenty-three after Aaron arrived. The Bears suddenly were 36-24 and just 6½ games out of first place.

Aaron's photo appeared in the *Telegram* for the first time on June 28. The posed image showed him tossing a ball to second baseman Bob MacConnell. The caption read: "$25,000 Keystone Combination. Performing at the Bears keystone are shortstop Hank Aaron and second baseman Bob MacConnell worth $25,000 to the parent Boston Braves. Aaron received $10,000 to leave the Indianapolis Clowns of the Negro American League and join the Braves, while MacConnell reportedly received $15,000 for signing after graduating from Brown University." Aaron's $10,000 went to the owner of the Clowns, of course; Aaron arrived in Eau Claire almost penniless. The photo ran with a story about the Fargo-Moorhead Twins defeating the Bears 7–5 on Friday night in front of 1,501 fans, thanks to half of the "Keystone Combination": Aaron committed an error that allowed a crucial run to score.

For a while that night Aaron must have experienced déjà vu. Many of the fans waited out a ninety-minute rain delay to see the Bears as well as Max Patkin, described as a "loose-limbed, crane-necked" baseball comedian. Patkin spent three innings performing his tricks, such as falling on his face while walking with an armload of bats, running backward from home to third while trying to reach base, and contorting his body while coaching at first and third base during the early innings. The former minor league pitcher for Green Bay in the Wisconsin State League had performed in front of the Cleveland Indians crowd only five days earlier. For five years, he had entertained exclusively for the Indians and the Saint Louis Browns, then owned by maverick Bill Veeck. Patkin was the first-base coach but was there to entertain the crowd and sometimes distract the opponents. For a brief time Patkin teamed with another baseball clown, Jackie Price. Boston Red Sox manager Lou Boudreau called them the "funniest show I ever saw." By the time his clowning days were over Patkin performed in front of more than two million people, including at least fifteen hundred patient baseball fans in Eau Claire and one Henry Aaron, a former baseball Clown.

As the team improved, the Carson Park crowds picked up. More than two thousand people turned out on June 30, a Monday, to see the Bears rout the Grand Forks Chiefs, 11–6. Aaron didn't disappoint the fans, hitting a home run and driving in three runs. His third hit of the night started a game-winning rally in the eighth inning, when the Bears scored six times to break a 5–5 tie. Pitcher Don Jordan had the game-winning hit, a two-run single.

The next evening was billed as Barnyard Nite with "plenty of fun, stunts, surprises, and laughs along with a good old-fashioned ball game." Eau Claire's farm team beat Grand Forks' farmhands again for a three-game sweep as Aaron hit a long double to center, scored twice, and stole two bases in the Bears' 4–2 win. In his first forty-five trips to the plate as an Eau Claire Bear, Aaron was 21-for-45. Not bad for a homesick eighteen-year-old.

On the Fourth of July Aaron showed just what kind of baseball fireworks his bat could provide. The Bears swept a doubleheader from the Saint Cloud Rox that day as Aaron had six hits in ten at bats. In the first game, the Bears were trailing 7–6 in the eighth inning when Aaron hit a grand slam to give them a 10–7 victory. The home run came off relief pitcher Art Rosser, whom Aaron had faced in his first at bat in Eau Claire. In the second game Aaron had a double and RBI as he went 4-for-5 in a 10–3 win. The sweep gave the Bears three wins in four games against the Rox and sent them home with something they hadn't had all season—momentum.

On Saturday, July 5, the Bears played the Duluth Dukes. An overflow crowd of 3,770 fans turned out to see the streaking Aaron and red-hot Bears—as well as the fireworks in the park after the game. But the Bears lost, 3–2. Aaron was 1-for-4 with a line drive double to left field.

Aaron was the talk not only of Eau Claire and the Northern League but of the Boston Braves' front office as well. Roland Hemond, an assistant scouting director, said Braves officials could hardly believe the reports

The stands of Carson Park stadium were filled to overflowing during the 1951 Northern League All-Star Game. Attendance was strong again in 1952, when Henry Aaron helped the Bears get back in the pennant race.

(Photo courtesy of the *Eau Claire Leader-Telegram*)

they were hearing about Aaron. "It was amazing. He hit the ball so well at Eau Claire. He came in midseason without any spring training and started knocking the cover off the ball." Braves scout Billy Southworth turned in such a glowing description of Aaron's play that "everybody got excited. My gosh, he's got a chance to be a great hitter," Hemond said, remembering the talk among Braves officials. After Southworth's visit, Braves farm director John Mullen came to Eau Claire himself for a week to see the phenom. Hemond remembers it well because during one game he placed an urgent call to Mullen during a Bears game. Mullen left his seat at Carson Park to talk to Hemond, in the process missing a home run by Aaron. "I can laugh at it now because Henry hit so many more," said Hemond, who in 2000 was an assistant to the president for the Arizona Diamondbacks. Bears president Randall Bezanson said the Braves were so excited about Aaron that they called Eau Claire every day for updates. "Each time they insisted that our manager not try to alter any of Aaron's fielding habits or give him any hitting advice," Bezanson said.

Aaron's hitting style confused and amazed umpire Ham Olive. In one game against Fargo, Aaron had a 1-1 count. "The next pitch was a mile high. The catcher started to jump up to catch it, and I called it a ball. I got a terrifically loud voice—you could hear me for miles—and everybody heard me call a ball, and just as I yelled it, Hank took that bat straight up and down and hit it over the right field fence for a home run," Olive said. "I called many a strike on Hank that he hit. He was that quick. It was embarrassing when everyone would hear me call a pitch and him hit it."

Olive had two other distinctive memories of Aaron. "Only time I ever seen him strike out, I called him three and he said, 'Mr. Hambone'—that's what he called me—'is that three? I sure didn't know I had two strikes on me or I would hit it,'" Olive recalled Aaron saying. As a fielder, Aaron would leave his glove on the infield when he was up to bat, as was the custom then before a rule made it illegal. "If they was two out, he would cut loose from deep in the hole [at shortstop]. While the ball was goin' one way his glove'd be goin' the other and Hank was trottin' in to bat," Olive said.

Aaron's confidence continued to build in his first month as a Bear. On July 10, Aaron, Covington, and Bowers—along with two other Bears, Bill Adair as manager and Bobby Brown—were named to the Northern League All-Star team. Only twenty players were chosen for the squad from approximately 150 in the league that season.

The game was played July 16 in Superior in front of an overflow crowd of 5,318 fans who had paid one dollar a ticket. Some came to see Aaron, who had been described in a local newspaper as "easily the best prospect in the Northern League today." Aaron came into the game leading the league with a .374 average. His first time up he singled, then twisted his ankle trying to break up a double play at second base. Although he went by ambulance to the hospital and the injury kept him out of the lineup for a week, he had to feel good about himself. He could have read about the Major League All-Star Game played a few days earlier—when Hammerin' Hank Sauer and Jackie Robinson hit home runs for the National League, and Joe DiMaggio and Larry Doby, the first black player in the American League, starred for the losing team—and realized that he was good, would maybe be as good as them someday.

That was his dream—to be a star. Lew Coyer, who in 1952 was a thirty-seven-year-old factory worker at U.S. Rubber, has a story to prove it. Coyer often dropped off his son, Jim, at the ballpark before the game, then motored back across the lake to resume his work on the 3 to 11 P.M. shift. On occasion, when Coyer picked up Jim after the game, he gave Aaron, Covington, and Bowers a ride back downtown. Coyer sympathized with their loneliness in a town where everyone else had a permanent home. His parents died when he was thirteen, and afterward he lived at the YMCA for ten years. All alone, much like Aaron. "I'd do most of the talking. They weren't much for conversation, unless one of them had a sensational play or a home run," Coyer said of the three Bears. One night Aaron signed a ball for Jim Coyer. Jim eventually lost it in a neighborhood ball game when it rolled under a fence into the yard of a neighbor who wouldn't give it back, but he always wanted that ball back because Aaron wrote more than his name on it. He signed it, "Someday I'll be a big shot—Henry Aaron."

Along with being named to the All-Star team on July 10, Aaron got another taste of being a hero on July 13. The Bears and Sioux Falls Canaries were tied 4–4 going into the bottom of the ninth. Two men were on base when Aaron came up. As was his custom when he reached the batter's box, Aaron pulled the bat up between his legs into his crotch to clean it off, whether it was dirty or not. He then cleanly hit the first pitch from Gordon Van Dyke 350 feet on a line over the left-center-field fence and onto the adjoining football field. It was Aaron's sixth homer of the season. More than 780 professional home runs later, Aaron would connect with that ball again, this time with his hands. Bill Anderson, the fifteen-year-old Bears volunteer, was sitting along third base when the ball cleared the fence and landed in the football field. He was the first one to get to it. In the excitement over the homer, team officials forgot to ask for the ball back. Anderson put it in a drawer at home along with Bears and Braves mementos from those years. When Aaron returned in 1994 to dedicate the statue, Anderson brought along the ball, now a sepia brown and still mud-stained from its hard landing. After Aaron's speech at the statue dedication, Anderson fished the ball out of his suit coat pocket and handed it over to Aaron's escort with the message that if Aaron wanted it, he could keep it. If not, would he sign it? Aaron listened to the story while riding in a limousine on his way out of town. He took the ball in his hands and rolled it over a few times, at once wondering if it really meant anything to him now among the thousands of mementos he has, and yet appreciating the sentiment of holding an object that marked the start of his baseball odyssey. A lifetime had gone by since, as was the league custom, an umpire had rubbed that ball with Georgia mud before the game to condition the leather and hurled it toward Aaron as an early test of his hitting skills. He knew he had passed the test. Over and over and over. To hold the ball again, to remember its history as a symbol of his origins—that was enough for him that day. He signed the ball and asked the escort to return it to Anderson.

MAKING FRIENDS

Once he got his bearings in 1952 Aaron began to meet people and enjoy his stay in Eau Claire. On Sunday nights he went to the Clell and Joyce Buzzell house where he ate dinner, played with their children, and became a family friend. "I met a lot of my friends in Eau Claire. I had an open invitation to a lot of homes for dinner and even for breakfast," Aaron said. "I got along very well back in Eau Claire. The people treated me fine."

One of them was Trudy Johnson, a friendly twenty-six-year-old waitress at the Paradise Cafe. Like most people in Eau Claire, she found it exciting to associate with professional baseball players, no matter what their color, even though she wasn't a baseball fan until the Bears began frequenting the Paradise. The players felt so comfortable at the Paradise that they wrote letters back home while waiting for their $1.25 dinners to arrive—T-bone steaks, potatoes, salad, and toast. The café was owned by John Speros and located one block from the YMCA on Gibson Street, across the street from Dixie Cream Glazed Donuts. As Johnson recalls, "The café was run by Greeks, and they came from the old school where everyone is welcome. We were nice to them, and I think they always appreciated that. As he kept getting better and better, I was always reminding people that I waited on Hank Aaron."

Aaron enjoyed going to movies when he had time. The early 1950s was a great time to dream of being famous. The big screen (and the suddenly popular little television screen) was filled with big names. One block from the YMCA, the State theater was screening Humphrey Bogart in *High Sierra*, Bette Davis in *Another Man's Poison,* and James Stewart and Rock Hudson in *Bend of the River*. Down the street at the Hollywood were Dean Martin and Jerry Lewis in *Jumping Jacks* and Robert Mitchell and Jane Russell in *His Kind of Woman*. None of the stars was black, but Aaron was beginning to realize that because of Jackie Robinson a person could be black and become somebody in the United States.

Aaron eventually became comfortable moving about and being him-self—the new himself—in Eau Claire. Before games Aaron and team-mates occasionally relaxed on the banks of placid Half Moon Lake, which surrounds the municipal Carson Park in the middle of the city, and fished for largemouth bass, sunfish, and bluegills. He was seen about town with a comic book sticking out of his back pocket. Walking to and from the stadium, the Bears crossed a causeway and bridge over the lake. At the far end of the causeway was the Parkway refreshment stand. The ten-foot-wide walk-up food store sold Richardson's Root Beer on tap for five cents a mug, hot dogs, hot beef sandwiches, Dolly Madison ice cream, malted milks, and "ice cold pop." Bears players often stopped there for lunch after a morning practice.

John Schaaf remembers playing baseball on an empty lot near the stand when Aaron and several teammates came by. Aaron had a ball sticking out of the back pocket of his uniform and came up to young Schaaf and asked if he'd like it signed. Schaaf eagerly accepted it and put it on his bedroom dresser. Later that summer, the ball accidentally found its way from Schaaf's house into one of the neighborhood sandlot games. Some-one tagged a pitch for a home run and sent the Henry Aaron autographed ball to a watery grave in Half Moon Lake.

The Bears lived either at the downtown YMCA or on the lower west side, across the Grand Avenue bridge over the Chippewa River. Players who lived downtown picked up teammates, such as rookie infielder Johnny Goryl, on the way to the ballpark. In that way Aaron began to meet some young women who were his age. Mary Golden, Susan Hauck, Carol Bridges, and Dorothy Ostberg all were eighteen, recent graduates of Eau Claire high schools, and neighbors. They also were Bears fans—"Everybody went to the ball games," Golden said—and eventually struck up conversations when they saw the Bears walk by their houses. People called them "baseball Annies," "dugout daisies," or just plain groupies. When the players and girls became friendly, they went across the street to the red brick Randall School on Fifth Avenue and Hudson Street where they played basketball by moonlight or sat in the schoolyard swings and talked in the dark where few people would have seen them.

With his square jaw and outgoing personality, Covington had no trouble drawing the attention of the foursome of flirtatious eighteen-year-old women. Aaron "stayed in the back and was very quiet. He'd go along with everybody else," Mary Golden said. None of the girls thought they were doing anything wrong by making friends with young black men, and none of their parents interfered. "Nobody really paid attention to the color," Golden said. Skin color was such a nonissue with the young women that they even laughed at Aaron because in the dark "all you could see was his eyes," Golden said.

Aaron eventually drew closer to one of the women, Sue Hauck, and her family. "She was kind of funny and comical, and that's probably why Hank would talk to her more. She was easy for him to talk to," Golden said. Hauck had just graduated from Saint Patrick's High School, which was adjacent to a Roman Catholic parish about a half-mile from the stadium. She liked Aaron's quiet, gentlemanly personality and "just loved that southern accent."

Aaron soon became a regular at the Arnold and Blanche Hauck residence, a modest two-story, two-gabled home at 516 Hudson Street. During the days of the butch haircut, Arnold Hauck became known as Butch. He owned Butch's Barber Shop at the downtown Hotel Eau Claire, the city's most respected inn and eatery because it came recommended by the famous chef Duncan Hines, according to the hotel's ads. "I might not have said fifty words all summer if it wasn't for Wes and Julie and a white family that sort of adopted me," Aaron said. Aaron felt comfortable at the Haucks', comfortable enough to sit and hold hands with Sue on the small, screened-in front porch or to walk right in the house as though he were one of the family. "It was an important relationship for me to have a family take me into their heart, to make me feel welcome," Aaron said.

Aaron and Hauck didn't date, but they spent many evenings talking, for the affable Sue was able to get Aaron to open up a little and relax. With her dark brown hair, slender build on a five-feet-seven frame, and bubbly personality, it was easy to see why Aaron was attracted to her. Besides all that, she was athletic too, once winning a softball throw contest for boys and girls. She had a full-time job doing bookkeeping and secretarial work, and in the evenings she and her girlfriends went to the stadium to watch the Bears play. Sue kept her eye on Henry, no matter what other people thought. "It was never a romance. It was a friendship," Sue said. "I suppose people thought we were dating. I liked him. I guess you could say I was infatuated with him. Back then if you would talk with a black person you were awful. I used to think that was wrong. I was never raised that way."

Aaron ate meals with the Haucks, and Arnold and Blanche were proud to have him in their home. The Haucks had five children, five bedrooms, and no place for bigotry. When Bruton was the city's first black ballplayer in 1950, he too had come to the Haucks to visit. He was friends with Sue's older sister, Jeanne, and people talked, but the Haucks didn't care.

One of the few black residents in Eau Claire at the time worked at Butch Hauck's barbershop as a shoe shiner. One day a prominent banker being trimmed by Butch asked why he had hired a black man, but he used a derogatory term. Butch Hauck became enraged but maintained control. Though he was only halfway through the banker's haircut he quickly threw off the apron and said the cut was done. The banker complained. Butch answered, "It's never going to get done in here. Get the hell out." When Butch was a young boy in Willmar, Minnesota, the Ku Klux Klan had persecuted his family because they were Catholic. He never forgot what it felt like to be treated that way, and it's probably why he stood up for blacks in Eau Claire, his son Steve Hauck said. It probably also explains why Sue Hauck never thought twice about holding hands with a young black man on her front porch.

Holding hands with a white girl and eating in white folks' houses—
Aaron was hundreds of miles from the Mason and Dixon Line and seeing
another side of America. His world was opening up. He was going to go
places in his life, and most of them would be better than the South he
knew as a child. "Playing in Eau Claire gave me a chance to look at
things with a much broader, wider scope. I learned you have to judge
people individually rather than collectively," he said. "I was treated as
fair as could be."

Aaron's scariest moment in Eau Claire came while in the company of
Sue Hauck and her friends. One night the women and ballplayers drove
thirteen miles west of Carson Park to the village of Elk Mound, so named
because it was on an upland prairie where herds of elk used to graze. The
mound is on the edge of Elk Mound. A winding road leads a half-mile to
the top, where a twenty-foot-high stone and mortar tower is perched. In
recent years a memorial plaque was installed outside the entrance. It reads:
"In memory of the deceased rural letter carriers of Dunn County." Metal
steps on the inside lead to an observation deck. Visitors to the mound during the day have a 360-degree view of the surrounding forests and farmland for ten miles or more and an intimate view of the heavens at night.

Sue Hauck, Aaron, and their friends, about eight in all, piled into a
couple of cars and drove up for the scenic overlook. Some of the women's
white male friends heard about the outing and decided to follow. Apparently the men had grown jealous of the black ballplayers and wanted to
see what really was happening between them and the women. While on
the hill, the women saw the men's car coming and became frightened. The
women weren't ashamed that they were with Aaron and Covington, but
they suspected the white men were ready to put up their fists over it. "We
didn't want them to know who we were with. We didn't want to cause any
trouble, so the ballplayers went and hid in the bushes," Mary Golden said.

The ruse worked. The men turned around at the top and headed back
down the hill after seeing only the women. Aaron and Covington came
out of hiding. The fear and excitement of the moment made a lasting
impression on Aaron. In 1994, as he left Eau Claire by airplane after the
statue dedication at Carson Park, he asked where Elk Mound was. The village, just a break in the cornfields when viewed from above, was pointed
out and Aaron took a long look until it disappeared from his view. As
a celebrity and promoter of equal opportunities for blacks, Aaron was

probably glad that he didn't have to fight his first racial battle with his hands atop Elk Mound, Wisconsin. If he had, all bets would have been on the man with the quick wrists and his powerful, 205-pound friend.

ONE OF THE BEARS

The Eau Claire Bears, as it turned out, may have been the perfect team for Aaron in his first season. Not only did it have two other black ball-players in a city where they didn't have to break the color barrier, but it also had a mix of players about Aaron's age, such as Johnny Goryl, Ken Reitmeier, and Bobby Brown, along with several players in their twenties: Elmer Toth, Julie Bowers, George Kornack, Lantz Blaney, and Bob MacConnell. Kornack and Blaney had just returned from service in the Korean War. Blaney was a member of the U.S. Army 111th Airborne. Aaron was worried for a time that he might be drafted (he wasn't). Goryl, also eighteen, joined the Bears after Aaron in late June.

Goryl was impressed by the way Aaron grabbed any bat of any length or weight off the rack and often hit with a different bat each time up, paying little attention to what he had in his hands. "He could hit with anything. He had tremendous eye-hand coordination," said Goryl, a native of Cumberland, Rhode Island, who eventually made it to the majors with the Chicago Cubs (1957–59) and Minnesota Twins (1962–64) and was still in baseball at the turn of the century as an infield coach with the Cleveland Indians. He briefly managed the Twins in 1980 and 1981.

The Bears player-manager, Bill Adair, turned out to be one of Aaron's favorites. At first, however, Aaron was concerned when he found out that Adair was also from Mobile. He knew that white people didn't give blacks a fair chance back in Mobile, and he wondered how Adair would treat him. It turned out that Adair treated all his players alike. Adair missed his chance to play in the majors because of his service in World War II, so he became a career minor league manager—he was a teacher at heart—and won numerous pennants around the country. In fact, the pennant with the Bears in 1951 was his third straight. Adair eventually was reunited with Aaron twice in the Major Leagues as an assistant with the 1962 Milwaukee Braves and with the 1967 Atlanta Braves. In 1970 Adair briefly realized his dream of coaching in the majors when he managed the Chicago White Sox, winning four games out of ten.

Adair was supposed to have an assistant coach for at least part of 1952, the famous and infamous Charlie Root. A team press release early that season said that Root had joined the 1952 staff, yet no players recall Root being with the team that season. Root was an assistant coach for the Chicago Cubs from 1951 through 1953, then came to Eau Claire in 1954 as the team's head coach. In 1927 Root won twenty-six games for the Chicago Cubs. He pitched in four World Series with the Cubs and had a 201-60 career record, but he was most famous for a home run that Babe Ruth hit off him in the 1932 World Series. The home run is known as Ruth's "called shot." Ruth allegedly pointed to center field before hitting the home run

Henry Aaron, far left in the middle row, was the starting shortstop for the Eau Claire Bears at age eighteen. Other members of the team that year were, left to right in the front row, Bill Conroy, Johnny Goryl, Bobby Brown, Don Jordan, and Joe Subbiondo; second row, Aaron, Don Auten, Charles Doehler, player-manager Bill Adair, Lantz Blaney, George Kornack, and Julie Bowers; back row, Chester Morgan (out of uniform because he was injured), Dick Engquist, Elmer Toth, Gordon Roach, Wes Covington, Bob MacConnell, and Ken Reitmeier.

(Photo courtesy of the *Eau Claire Leader-Telegram*)

to that spot. The home run is often cited as an example that Ruth was so fabulously talented that he could hit a home run not only when he wanted but where he wanted.

In 1954, when Eau Claire players teased him about the home run, Root said Ruth never called the shot, that he was just pointing at Cubs players who were baiting him. "If you'd mention that to [Root] in batting practice, he'd knock you down," said Johnny Goryl, who also played for Root's

Bill Adair was the player-manager for the Eau Claire Bears in 1952. He was from the same city, Mobile, Alabama, as rookie shortstop Henry Aaron.

(Photo courtesy of the *Eau Claire Leader-Telegram*)

Charlie Root, the Chicago Cubs pitcher who was haunted by one of Babe Ruth's most famous home runs, coached the Eau Claire Braves in 1954 and later coached Henry Aaron with the Milwaukee Braves.

(Photo courtesy of the *Eau Claire Leader-Telegram*)

Bears in 1954. During rain delays, Root sometimes would talk about the famous batters he had faced. A young Bears player, unaware of Root's history, once asked him if he ever had pitched against the great Babe Ruth. The irascible Root rose from his seat, slowly walked over to the player, and spat tobacco juice all over his face. After twenty years, Root had had enough of the needling, enough of discussing the one pitch that no one could seem to forget.

In 1956 Root was named pitching coach for the Milwaukee Braves, who had a pennant-contending team with Aaron and Covington, two former Eau Claire rookies. By observing Root, Aaron would have learned his first lesson about the untouchable Babe Ruth: If you mess with a legend, be prepared.

Although Aaron didn't talk or socialize much with the other Bears players, he was respected, said Chester Morgan, the teammate who was on second base when Aaron stroked his first two minor league hits. Aaron wasn't treated any differently because he was black. "I don't remember anybody from our team or other teams giving blacks a hard time," Morgan said. "Henry was accepted all the time. He was a ballplayers' ballplayer. There wasn't anything not to like about Henry. Henry had class from Day One." Morgan grew up in Greenville, Mississippi, in the Deep South like Aaron. He saw racism firsthand, but he learned as a white person how to overcome it firsthand. Morgan was raised on a cotton farm along the Mississippi River, and many of his coworkers and friends were black. They went about their work and paid little attention to skin color, much like the Northern League players in 1952.

With three dollars a day for meals, long road trips, and three months of being together day after day, the 1952 Eau Claire Bears learned how to stay loose and have fun. "We ate a lot of hamburgers—and peanut butter. You could put peanut butter in your suitcase," Morgan said. Goryl was nicknamed "Groucho" because he "had one of the best Groucho Marx imitations of all-time," Ken Reitmeier said. The team had a radio in the dugout and listened to broadcasts of the game they were playing, occasionally taking umbrage at some unfair remark by the play-by-play announcer, sometimes banging their heads on the low, pitched dugout roof after a big play. Many of the Bears loved to play pool, including Aaron. Bowers was so good that he could have made a living at it, Reitmeier said. During one road trip to Saint Cloud, a Bears pitcher started up a vintage Model T car that was on display at a city lot and drove it up the steps of the county courthouse. "That got us in a good bit of trouble," Reitmeier said. Reitmeier and one of the veteran players, Elmer Toth, occasionally stopped at the Gordon Hotel, where they could buy ten-cent beers. Toth remembers that in Eau Claire he enjoyed some of that "good Wisconsin beer."

Toth had been around. A native of Perryopolis, Pennsylvania, in 1950 he pitched in the Class B Southern League in Jackson, Mississippi, and in 1951 in Hartford and Atlanta in Class AA and A ball. He thought he was on his way to the majors in 1952 when he started the season with the Milwaukee Brewers of the American Association in Class AAA, but he was sent to Evansville, Indiana. He hurt his arm there while throwing in relief. He pitched sidearm, which put more strain on the shoulder, and hadn't warmed up properly. He was sent down further to Eau Claire to rehabilitate his arm, which he did by pitching sparingly and by renting a boat and—elbows akimbo—rowing around Half Moon Lake, all six feet four, 190 pounds of him.

Reitmeier wore the same number, twenty-one, as his hero and fellow southpaw, Warren Spahn of the Braves. Reitmeier had his most memorable day of the season in Grand Forks. The Bears were scheduled to play a split doubleheader against the Chiefs, but when the first game got rained out he and Toth headed to a bar for a couple of hours, expecting the games to be postponed. After several glasses of beer they lost track of time. Then a man came into the bar and said the games were underway. Reitmeier and Toth hailed a cab and rushed to the stadium halfway through the first game, making up an excuse when they saw manager Bill Adair. He must have believed them—or didn't get close enough to smell their breath. Adair started the wobbly Reitmeier at pitcher in the second game and not only did he win the game, he got three hits.

One of the true veterans on the Bears roster that season was pitcher George Kornack. After playing in Owensboro, Kentucky, in 1950, Kornack served in the army as a tank commander in Korea in 1951. He was discharged in October of that year after being shot in the buttocks by the enemy with a machine gun. "They used to call me 'shot in the ass,'" Kornack said. When he returned home at age twenty-one he was happy to be assigned to the Eau Claire Bears. Although he was far from home, the native of Chelsea, Massachusetts, was comfortable in Eau Claire because the 1952 Bears got along well, even though they came from all parts of the United States and Canada. "We didn't have any problems on that team racially," Kornack said. "It was a good bunch of guys."

His favorite memory of Aaron was when the young shortstop booted a ground ball that should have been an easy out while Kornack was on the mound. "Aaron said to me, 'Don't worry. I'll take care of it.' And he did. He came up to bat and hit a shot over the left field fence." The images of Aaron's line drive hits and the little dip of his hip just before swinging ("that's where he got all his power") are burned into Kornack's memory. Aaron once hit a sizzling line drive toward the shortstop, who jumped up to catch it only to turn around and see the ball keep carrying and carrying until it went over the outfield fence.

PENNANT, BATTING TITLE SLIP AWAY

Things kept looking up for Aaron and the Bears. They had several players with high batting averages and solid starting pitching. Aaron was consistent at the plate but could just as quickly make an error and throw a game. For example, on July 20 and 21, he went 6-for-12 in two victories at Aberdeen. He was one of the heroes in the July 21 game when he singled and scored the go-ahead run in the fifteenth inning as the Bears won a 9–5 marathon that ended just before the 11:50 P.M. curfew. The next day, July 22, he committed a two-out error in the seventh inning that cost the Bears the game.

Aaron looked like a sure thing to a lot of scouts, but hundreds of "sure things" never got out of the minor leagues for a variety of reasons, such as homesickness, poor work habits, bad attitudes, drinking problems, injury problems, romantic entanglements, marriage, the Korean War, or lack of desire to stick out the tough conditions for low pay in a seasonal job. Or they realized they just weren't going to make it in the majors. In late May, just one month into the season, Saint Cloud Rox pitcher Bob Mallon decided to quit baseball because he had been offered a job as a police officer in New York City, his hometown. He had walked twice as many batters as he had struck out that season and realized he needed to make another career choice. Yet Mallon, like every player in the Northern

League, was in the minors because at one time he had faith in himself. Nowhere is a dream tested more than in the minors, where players have only themselves to rely on day after day. "I have to believe every ballplayer, deep in his heart, thought, 'I know I can make it,'" Reitmeier said.

Still, they all lived on the edge of their dugout seats. Many players faithfully read the *Sporting News*, which reported the movement of all players up and down the baseball ladder. "Guys carried the *Sporting News* around in their back pockets and watched things like a hawk," Reitmeier said. Players knew that one man's promotion or demotion in a team's farm system caused a ripple effect on all the parent club's other minor league rosters. "Those guys all knew who was going down and who had to go," Reitmeier said. "They were very astute." And worried.

Making the majors required all-out effort. Eau Claire fans remembered how in 1952 and 1953 catcher Julie Bowers gave 100 percent every time a ground ball was hit to the infield. At the crack of the bat, he sprang off his haunches, flipped off his mask, and dug his cleats into the clay all in one motion. Then he sprinted in his shin guards down the first base line in foul territory, usually beating the runner and the ball to first base in order to back up the throw. He did it because that was baseball back then—you did the little things, made the extra effort whenever possible to give yourself a little better chance at making the majors.

Aaron was impressive but still had a lot of proving to do. What would he have thought if someone told him that thirty years later, on July 21, 1982, he would be standing on the steps of the Hall of Fame in Cooperstown about to be inducted? He might have said, "I told you I was going to be a big shot someday."

The Bears were a solid team with a mix of veteran players and several promising rookies, including Aaron, Reitmeier, and Goryl. Having young players meant ups and downs for the Bears. On July 23 the Bears lost 1–0 at Saint Cloud when Reitmeier walked home the game's only run. Saint Cloud player-manager Charlie Fox faked a steal of home from third base, causing the left-handed Reitmeier to hold up his delivery. Reitmeier was out-Foxed by an old pro. Fox played briefly in the majors, for the 1942 New York Giants, but he endured as a manager. Fox managed the San Francisco Giants from 1970 through 1974 and later managed the Montreal Expos and the Chicago Cubs. His Giants won the 1971 National League West title with Willie Mays, Willie McCovey, and Juan Marichal.

The day after Reitmeier's mistake, however, Bobby Brown, a young left-hander from Brooklyn had a memorable performance when he pitched two complete seven-inning games. The Bears won a doubleheader 6–2 and 5–0 as Brown gave up only seven hits in the fourteen innings. Brown had driven to Eau Claire in a canary yellow Packard convertible, but he proved he wasn't all show. A grand slam by Covington, his fourth of the season, gave the Bears the edge in the opening game.

On August 1 Aaron still led the league with a .359 batting average, with Covington close behind at .335. On August 4 the Bears swept a double-header from Fargo-Moorhead and moved into second place with a 58-38 record, nine games behind the new first-place team, Superior. In the twin bill, Aaron had a two-run double and a three-run home run. He was more than a natural. Aaron was consistent, playing like a veteran at age eighteen; he kept coming at you.

The next night, Covington was knocked unconscious by a pitch and taken to Luther Hospital, where he remained for two weeks. Covington's injury helped kill the Bears' pennant hopes in mid-August. But his wasn't the only head injury that had the Bears aching. Third baseman Johnny Goryl lost a pop fly in the sun; it hit him on the top of the head and knocked him out. He was out of action briefly. First baseman Dick Engquist suffered a broken nose and went on the disabled list. Two players were suspended, catcher Don Auten and pitcher Gordon Roach. Auten, who started the season at Evansville, had already missed games in early July when a batter hit him on the head while following through on a swing. The Bears were so shorthanded that they had to use three pitchers as infielders. Player-manager Bill Adair was forced into starting. They lost five straight games on a South Dakota road trip to Sioux Falls and Aberdeen and again fell nine games behind Superior with two weeks to play.

The loss of Engquist was Aaron's fault. While warming up for the August 11 game in Aberdeen, Aaron was swinging a bat left-handed because he had been considering trying to become a switch-hitter. Engquist, a six-feet-four, 210-pound first baseman from Detroit, was standing nearby when the bat slipped from Aaron's hands and hit him in the face. He suffered a badly broken nose and Aaron a badly bruised ego. Aaron, who had natural left-handed ability, became upset by his mistake—the Chuck Wiles injury still was on his mind—and immediately gave up the idea of switch-hitting. Early in his Major League career he regretted the decision, realizing he probably could have been an effective switch-hitter. He held the bat cross-handed when he learned to hit as a right-hander, so he was already used to gripping the bat like a left-handed hitter. In the end, the Engquist accident may have helped Aaron break Ruth's record. As a switch-hitter, Aaron probably never would have been as consistent a home run hitter in the majors as he was hitting just right-handed.

The banged-up Bears returned home from the disastrous road trip for a two-game home series against Duluth on August 13 and 14. They defeated the Dukes 7–5 in the first game as Aaron went 2-for-3 with a double. The action the next night included a performance by Jackie Price, who billed himself as "baseball's one-man acrobatic clown show." Having come from the famous Indianapolis Clowns only months before, Aaron knew all about baseball comedy. But it was unlikely that the remorseful Aaron and the suddenly reeling Bears were in any mood to laugh. They lost 9–4 to Duluth in front of 1,993 Carson Park fans. Aaron had three singles in five at bats and committed an error. The Bears then headed north for three games to Superior, where the fans still hadn't forgotten what Aaron did to Wiles. The Bears lost two out of three, but Aaron was 6-for-12 in the series.

The Bears and Aaron didn't go down without some fun, however. On August 26 in Saint Cloud, several players took part in athletic competitions on East Side Night before their last game of the season against the Rox. Outfielder Lantz Blaney of the Bears won the seventy-five-yard dash, edging out Aaron and two Saint Cloud players. The muscular Blaney had been a four-sport star in high school in Morgantown, West Virginia. In a timed event to see who could run the bases the fastest, Aaron lost again, this time to Wayne Heim of Saint Cloud. Manager Charley Fox of Saint Cloud won the accuracy-throwing contest for catchers. Even if Aaron wasn't the fastest man on the field, he still impressed the *Saint Cloud Times* writer, who referred to him as the Bears' "sensational shortstop."

The night of festivities included calliope music provided by Lakeland Bakeries for the 711 fans at Municipal Stadium (an average crowd for the Rox, who drew only about 45,000 for the season). The Bears won 3–2, no thanks to Aaron who was 0-for-3 and struck out twice in a game for only the second time all year. The win was the Bears' sixth in seven games, but it was too late. They still were nine games behind Superior with seven to play.

Not even a no-hitter by Gordon Roach was enough to rescue the Bears. After returning home to Carson Park, Roach and the Bears beat Aberdeen 10–1 on August 28. Roach let only one ball get out of the infield, but a walk and a wild pitch let the lone run score.

The Bears had been mathematically eliminated from the pennant race the night before.

chapter 2

EAU CLAIRE BASEBALL

The Bears' pennant hopes disappeared late in the 1952 season along with Aaron's hopes for the batting crown. When the players turned in their uniforms and scattered and Carson Park stadium was shut down for another winter, the summer of 1952 appeared to be just another season in the long history of baseball in Eau Claire: A winning team, good fan support, some Major League prospects to root for, and hope for next year. Looking back, however, Aaron's presence that season probably made it the most significant one in Eau Claire baseball history. Never before and never again would the city help mold anyone—as a baseball player and as a person—who ultimately made such an impact at the national level.

Yet Aaron's experience in Eau Claire wouldn't have happened—the way for him would not have been prepared—without the eighty-five years of city baseball that preceded him. Blacks had played baseball in Eau Claire as early as the 1880s, almost as early as anywhere in the country, but there was a time in the early 1900s when they weren't welcome in Eau Claire—or in most other places.

BEFORE HENRY

The National Association of Baseball Players was organized in 1858 with sixteen New York teams, and by the mid-1860s baseball was becoming a popular new form of recreation. Many soldiers played baseball in their

Civil War camps. When the war ended, soldiers returning to the Midwest spread the word about the game on empty sandlots in developing cities. By 1865, as Johnny went marching home, the number of teams had grown to 91, and by 1867 the number had more than doubled to 237.

Eau Claire was one of the cities that helped baseball earn the nickname "America's pastime." When many of its native sons returned from places like Chickamauga, Atlanta, and Vicksburg, mixed in with the veterans' tales of battles was mention of a diversion called baseball. A local newspaper editor heard the talk and wrote, "This national game is becoming so important that Eau Claire needs a club, to keep up with the times." Two years after the war ended, in September 1867, the first organized game in Eau Claire took place (no one recorded the score). Eau Claire actually was behind the times in Wisconsin. That same year, the first state baseball tournament was held with nine teams from Wisconsin and twenty teams total; Eau Claire was not among them.

The name for Eau Claire's first team, the Clearwater Boys, was appropriate. Eau Claire was named by French voyageurs—fur traders—in the spring of 1767, about eighty years before it began to grow into a city. The voyageurs, several Chippewa Indians, and a Chippewa chief were paddling log dugouts called *pirogues* for Englishman Jonathan Carver, who was mapping the region for the king of England. In 1778 Captain Carver, who had fought in the French and Indian wars, detailed his explorations in *Travels through the Interior Parts of North-America.* On their way up what is now the Chippewa River, the expedition noticed that a river flowing into the Chippewa from the east was clear. The Chippewa River had been running muddy, and the Frenchmen were ecstatic to find clear drinking water, exclaiming, "Eau Claire! Eau Claire!" They named it *La Rivière del' Eau Claire,* the River of Clear Water. The confluence of the two rivers became the center of the city of Eau Claire in the 1840s when a mill was built.

In 1868, 101 years after Carver passed by, the first recorded baseball game in Eau Claire took place when the city Lonestars defeated the west side Crocodiles, 92–87. It was far from the game we know today. The mound was forty-five feet from home plate—not sixty feet six inches—and the pitchers threw underhanded. Beginning in 1871 batters could call for the type of pitch they wanted, high or low. Pitchers could take a running start before they threw. Catchers' masks hadn't been invented, nor had fielding gloves.

Professional baseball began in 1869 with the Cincinnati Red Stockings, and in 1884—the same year as the first true World Series—it reached Eau Claire. That year the Eau Claire team had two professionals, a pitcher and a catcher, and played against teams from Chicago, Green Bay, and Chippewa Falls, as well as Minnesota teams from Minneapolis, Saint Paul, Winona, and Stillwater. In midsummer the Eau Claire Crescents defeated the Saint Paul Red Caps so soundly, 12–0, that the *Daily Leader* said they could "give any club in this section of the country, whether league or not, a lively tussle." The Crescents' professional pitcher struck out seventeen batters.

Early that season the local newspaper reported that Eau Claire was to be part of the Northwestern League, but it apparently wasn't one of the league's original twelve teams. Eau Claire played many of the Northwestern League teams that season, but the games may have been for exhibition purposes only. The league was considered one of the four strongest in the nation that year, along with the National League, the American Association, and the Eastern League. For example, eleven of Stillwater's twenty-seven players went on to play in the Major Leagues.

The 1884 team from Stillwater—the Stillwaters—had the first professional black ballplayer in history, Bud Fowler. He was also a barber in Stillwater. Born in Cooperstown, New York, in 1854, he had played pro ball for twelve years in small cities around the country prior to Stillwater, and was known for his pitching, hitting, and catching. When Stillwater and the league folded by mid-August, Fowler left town and resurfaced in 1885 to play with a team in Keokuk, Iowa. Box scores in the baseball record of the time, *Sporting Life*, don't indicate that Fowler played against Eau Claire. In September of 1884 Eau Claire ended its season by playing Stillwater, but at that point Stillwater had all new players. It is possible, however, that Eau Claire played Stillwater in an unrecorded exhibition game before or during the season. Stillwater, on Minnesota's eastern border at the Saint Croix River, is close enough to Eau Claire—about seventy miles—to make a game between the teams feasible, and trains regularly ran through the region. On July 18, 1884, the *Leader* carried a box score between the Crescents and the Chippewas that showed a Fowler (no first name given) playing pitcher and right field. Was it Bud Fowler picking up a few dollars on the side in Chippewa Falls, Wisconsin?

That same season, Moses Fleetwood Walker played for Toledo and became the first black player in the Major Leagues. Fowler and Walker were two of about thirty black men who played in white leagues before the turn of the century and before Major League owners banned black players.

The 1884 season marked the beginning of pro baseball not only for Eau Claire but for Minneapolis and Saint Paul as well. The visiting teams arrived by the most modern form of transportation, the railroad, although they still might have been able to catch a stagecoach or a Chippewa River steamboat, of which there were fewer each year. In 1870 the arrival in Eau Claire of the first locomotive of the West Wisconsin Railroad was a grand event that had been fifteen years in the making. A throng of ten thousand people—more than the population of the city—as well as Wisconsin Governor Lucius Fairchild were on hand to watch it puff into town on its five-foot wheels and send steam curling into the hazy August sky. Four cars trailed, filled with passengers who hung their heads out the windows for the novelty of seeing the Chippewa River while on wheels. Two uniformed watchmen standing on the exit platform brought up the rear. Soon about seventy-five trains a day were coming to Eau Claire, bringing northern European immigrants who had crossed the Atlantic by ship and taken a train through the heartland. Trains ferried passengers across the Midwest, immigrants as well as traveling ballplayers like the Stillwaters and the Saint Paul Red Caps.

When baseball teams visited Eau Claire they were fed dinner and housed by their opponents. They stayed in places like the Galloway House, a three-story brick hotel with one hundred rooms and Turkish baths. In 1884 it was billed as the only hotel in the nation with electric lights (they arrived in the city in 1883), although in those days of slow-moving information a self-promoting hotelier could say almost anything he wanted and not be taken to court for false advertising by a competitor. The hotel had to be a welcome sight after playing on the rough fields of the day. One editor criticized the Crescents in 1884 for too many wild throws, saying "the ball was constantly being lost in barns and pigsties." Either the players had very, very wild arms or the field was, as they used to say, carved out of a cow pasture. After each game there was a prize for the victorious team—a baseball. Balls were expensive and scarce at the time—blame the pigsties—making it worth trying for the extra base, playing the extra inning, or arguing a call. The balls were so coveted that a team from Saint Paul once refused to pay up after a defeat; Eau Claire refused to play Saint Paul again until their day of reckoning.

By 1885 baseball seemed to be the root of all evil in Eau Claire. Pro players from throughout the state were on the city's team. The men not only played for money but they bet on the games and played on Sundays, upsetting the local Protestant clergy who cited a local "no Sunday baseball law." One Sunday in September a warrant was issued against the players, and a sheriff arrived at the diamond. The crowd dispersed and the game eventually moved north fifteen miles to Chippewa Falls. The Eau Claire team's cause probably wasn't helped by the fact that its opponent was the Chicago Gordons, an all-black team. The Sunday baseball issue festered for six years, finally easing in 1891 when the sides agreed that church services would be held at the ball park, a pregame blessing for the misguided. The issue flared again in 1894, forcing the Eau Claire team to fold and resulting in the disbanding of the shaky league.

Baseball was hardly the city's biggest social ill, however. In 1885 Eau Claire had more than twenty houses of prostitution among its eight thousand residents, a reflection of the main industry, the male-dominated lumbering business. With holding ponds and rivers and sawmills, Eau Claire was on a main supply route for the millions of board feet of white pine that were cut in the heavily forested north during the winter and floated south in the spring on the Chippewa River. The lonely sawyers spent the winters in the woods, then traveled downstream with the logs in the spring to work at the mills. Eau Claire had so many mills along the Chippewa that it became known as Sawdust City. With all the prostitutes, lonely lumbermen who drank at the city's ninety saloons—obviously before government got into the business of regulating liquor sales—and baseball players who didn't respect the Sabbath, Eau Claire may well have been Sodom or Gomorrah in the eyes of the Christians. The imbibers apparently outnumbered the teetotalers in Eau Claire for many years because in 1920 Eau Claire County was the only county in Wisconsin to vote against Prohibition.

The Christians might not have liked Sunday baseball, but they couldn't dispute that the city team was darn good. Eau Claire won thirty-seven of forty-two games in 1885 and claimed to be the state champion. The 1885 team is considered Eau Claire's first professional team, as opposed to the previous year's team on which just two players were paid. In 1885 teams in the Northwestern Baseball League could pay their players seventy-five dollars a month. But a report in the *Daily Free Press* that an Eau Claire player was being paid three hundred dollars a month angered other players in the league and area laborers. It was a salary that hard-working immigrant farmers and northwoods lumbermen couldn't fathom—just for playing ball, just for playing a game.

Included in Eau Claire's sterling season of 1885 was a win over the Chicago Gordons on the Fourth of July. What a sight that must have been, the all-black Gordons arriving by train in Eau Claire on Independence Day twenty years after the Civil War. Any war veterans in the crowd had to realize that their effort helped make it possible for the Gordons to play baseball and travel the country. The game and celebration was the must-attend event of the holiday as two thousand people—about one in every four city residents—turned out. The Gordons' way of life continued for nearly seventy more years, about the same amount of time it took for civil rights legislation to pass. A team similar to the Gordons still was traveling the country in 1952: the Indianapolis Clowns.

One of Eau Claire's early baseball stadiums was the Driving Park.
(Photo courtesy of Chippewa Valley Museum, Eau Claire, Wisconsin)

Long before Eau Claire was a founding member of the Northern League in 1933, long before Carson Park, the minor leagues, the national and local breaking of the color barrier and Henry Aaron, there was the Driving Park. At this city baseball diamond another future Hall of Famer found his game as a young man and went on to establish a direct link between Eau Claire and baseball's first home run king, Babe Ruth.

The original Northern League formed in 1908 and died in 1908. It became the Minnesota-Wisconsin League from 1909 to 1912, reappeared as the Northern League in 1913, and fell apart during World War I. Eau Claire joined the Minnesota-Wisconsin League in 1910 and took first place. A championship banner hung downtown for several years. Eau Claire's Dave Callahan hit .365 and stole fifty-two bases, the best in the nation among minor leaguers in both categories, according to *Total Baseball.* The United States had fifty-two minor leagues that year.

Carson Park's predecessor was the Driving Park, built in 1902 on the city's south side. Driving Park's covered grandstand seated about five hundred people, many of whom would have taken a streetcar to within a

block of the sprawling athletic complex. Photos show Model T Fords parked along the third-base line, close enough to smell the cut grass and hear the crack of the wooden bat as a ball headed toward a shoulder-high, wooden outfield wall. The park also had a horse racing track, football field, polo field, and track and field facilities.

Driving Park eventually was torn down for a housing development around 1926 as the city expanded after World War I and began pushing south toward prairie farmland above the river valley. But if you drive through the city's historic Third Ward neighborhood now, at least part of the Driving Park complex still is visible. The parallel streets of McKinley and Roosevelt are joined at the ends by two connecting curves—ostensibly turns three and four of the old race track. The developers never bothered to make street corners when they put in the homes. A stately Georgian-style brick mansion has a manicured hedge bordering half the curve, and bicycles and strollers now hug the leafy green rail along the homestretch. The infield area once had a judging tower and hundreds of

An Eau Claire team posed for an informal photograph at the
Driving Park in the early 1900s.

(Photo courtesy of Chippewa Valley Museum, Eau Claire, Wisconsin)

spectators who were held back by an uneven white picket fence; now it's home to bratwurst cookouts, thrift sales, and driveway basketball games.

It was in the Driving Park where Burleigh Grimes of Clear Lake, Wisconsin, got his start in pro baseball in 1912. Unlike Aaron's 1952 season, which propelled him to the majors two years later, Grimes's season in Eau Claire almost marked the ending as well as the beginning of his career.

In May of 1912 the eighteen-year-old farm boy left his home in Clear Lake and headed to Eau Claire, about sixty miles to the southeast. Grimes had played on a Clear Lake town team, coached by his father, and was recruited by Russ Bailey, longtime coach of the Eau Claire team, by then known as the Commissioners. Grimes made the roster at May tryouts, but from the start of the season, Minnesota-Wisconsin League, or the Minny League as it was called, seemed to be on shaky footing. The number of teams had been cut in half from eight in 1911 to just four in 1912. Eau Claire was joined by teams from Rochester, Winona, and La Crosse.

Grimes made his pro debut as a right fielder on May 16. He was 1-for-2 at the plate with a double against the Winona Pirates in Winona, Minnesota. On May 21 the rookie Grimes was named the starting pitcher for the Commissioners' home opener against Rochester. It was the first of many thousands of times he would take the mound in the next twenty-three years en route to the Baseball Hall of Fame. Grimes gave up one run in the first four innings at the Driving Park. Then he was pulled for a relief pitcher during a five-run Rochester fifth inning, according to accounts in the *Eau Claire Leader*. Although Grimes didn't get the loss, Eau Claire wound up losing 7–6.

Throughout May and June Grimes alternated as a pitcher and either right fielder or center fielder. He had a 2-3 pitching record and was hitting .323. His first career pitching win came on June 12, a six-hitter in a 6–4 win over Rochester at the Driving Park. He struck out five. Grimes also had three hits in four at bats, an early indication of his hitting ability. He went on to become one of baseball's best-hitting pitchers (hitting .248 for his career), one of the few to have his own signature model bat. A report in the *Leader* about Grimes's pitching performance said, "Grimes for Eau Claire had a lot of stuff and used it well." Presumably, by using the word *stuff* the reporter was referring to a pitch that would make Grimes famous—the spitter. It was his favorite pitch. Grimes, who retired in 1934, is still known as the last of the great spitball pitchers.

With Grimes's win, Eau Claire was 18–8 and atop the Minny League, but not for long. On June 21 the *Eau Claire Leader* reported having heard—but didn't want to believe—that the local team was in financial trouble: "Rumor has gained widespread circulation around the place the last few days to the effect that the team would not go on the road but disband. The club officials are at a loss to know who gave rise to this rumor and wish to make it known that it is wholly unfounded. No doubt it started from some malcontent who fails to appreciate the town's leading enterprise. It is true that the attendance at games thus far has not been any too good but Eau Claire is not entertaining the idea of withdrawing from the Minny."

Less than two weeks later, however, the rumor came true. On July 1 Eau Claire's team disbanded, withdrawing from the league after a 3–2 loss to Winona at the Driving Park. Not enough fans were attending games, and the players could no longer be paid. The game against Winona showed how little interest there was in the team. Fewer than a hundred fans from the city's population of twenty thousand had turned out for the battle between the league leader, Winona, and second place Eau Claire (28–14) on a Sunday afternoon.

A heavy black border surrounded a sports page article with the headings, "Eau Claire Fans Repudiate the Baseball Game" and "Eau Claire Enters Cemetery Lot." The report said, "Baseball locally has been unconscious since the opening of the season, and the expected end came yesterday.... Just what the players will do is a matter of conjecture. They are all dead broke. One had a toothache last evening and he dared not enter a dentist office for he feared a sign of 'If you can't pay you are not welcome.'"

Two months after coming to Eau Claire Grimes knew he could play baseball, but now he was broke and didn't have a team. He didn't go home, however. With twenty-five cents in his pocket, he traveled to Austin, Minnesota, which had a team in the Southern Minnesota League, according to Chuck Clark, a Grimes historian from Clear Lake. Grimes didn't find any openings on the roster, so he hung around as a team helper, a ball boy and water boy. He got his break one day during a doubleheader when Austin needed a second pitcher. Grimes pitched and got the win, thanks to one of his own home runs. "I knew that was it," Grimes told Clark of his chance to catch on with a new team. "The rest is history."

Grimes soon caught the eye of the Detroit Tigers and was assigned to their minor league team in Ottumwa, Iowa, in 1913. In 1914 he moved up to Class AA teams in Chattanooga, Tennessee, and Richmond, Virginia. He spent most of the year at Richmond, where he achieved a rare double feat, leading the league in hitting as well as pitching (with a 22–13 record).

In 1915 and 1916 he played for Birmingham, Alabama, winning thirty-seven games in two seasons. That was enough for the Pittsburgh Pirates; they called him up to the majors at the end of the 1916 season. Grimes made his Major League pitching debut at age twenty-two.

It was a long way from Clear Lake and a defunct baseball team in Eau Claire to the Major Leagues in Pittsburgh, but Burleigh Grimes finally was on his way. Grimes played nineteen years in the majors, won 270 games, and was inducted into the Hall of Fame in 1964.

Along the way, Grimes was witness to at least one—maybe the most talked about—of Babe Ruth's 714 career home runs. When Ruth hit the much-discussed "called shot" in the 1932 World Series, Grimes had a ring-side seat with the Chicago Cubs. Grimes was one of the Cubs players who

Spitball pitcher Burleigh Grimes of Clear Lake, Wisconsin, began his pro baseball career in Eau Claire in 1912 and made it all the way to the Baseball Hall of Fame.

(Photo courtesy of the *Eau Claire Leader-Telegram*)

uttered epithets and rolled lemons on the field to distract Ruth during the at bat. After two strikes, Ruth pointed a finger at the Chicago bench. "I've still got the big strike left," Ruth said, according to Grimes. Some people thought Ruth pointed to center field before hitting the homer to that spot. If he had done that, the Cubs' tough pitcher Charlie Root "would have knocked Ruth down [with a pitch]. . . . He never pointed to center. But he did in a sense call the shot because he was saying he had a third strike coming," Grimes told Clark.

After World War I Eau Claire joined another version of the Northern League. The new league soon collapsed, in 1922, but not without a lively final season in Eau Claire. The star pitcher, Earle "Kid" Dunfee, a mid-summer addition to the team, was beaned by an opposing pitcher's sinking emery ball. (An emery ball was a pitch using a ball whose cover had been scratched or roughed up to make it more lively.) It was thought that Dunfee's career was over after he went to a hospital in critical condition. For twenty years he had made a living pitching for town teams in the Upper Midwest and Canada. Then thirty-eight years old, the 155-pound southpaw relied on an assortment of curves and a blazing fastball that equaled, as the *Daily Telegram* crudely put it, the "coon pitchers" of the Chicago Union Giants. He chewed tobacco only during games but not so that he could throw a spitball, or so he said. He was 28–2 in 1922 when he went down with a gasp from the crowd. It was a shame, people thought, that such a talent could be lost with one errant pitch. He could run the hundred-yard dash in 10.5 seconds and was reported to be a man of "considerable means." The hospital reports were grim, and he was all but left for dead by the local fans. Certainly the fans didn't expect to see him on the mound ever again.

Two weeks to the day after the accident he walked back on the mound to wild applause. He was Lazarus in heavy wool. Eau Claire was playing upriver rival Chippewa Falls. Dunfee not only threw a seven-hit shutout in a 7–0 victory, but he struck out fifteen, didn't walk a batter, and was 1-for-4 at the plate. If it had happened in New York in the Major Leagues, it would have been hailed as one of the greatest comeback performances of all time. But it happened in the not-quite-minor-leagues in Eau Claire, Wisconsin. The news story was headed "Dunfee, As Good As Ever, Tames the Chippewas, 7–0," and led off with the sentence "You can't keep a good man down." The crowd that day was estimated at between sixteen hundred and two thousand, almost four times the stadium capacity. They sat in supplementary bleachers and stood along the foul lines to see the comeback "Kid."

Earle "Kid" Dunfee's battery mate the day he returned from his deathbed was George "Dutch" Gerner. Like Dunfee, Gerner had traveled a dusty baseball road before coming to Eau Claire. A twenty-seven-year-old bachelor who lived at the downtown YMCA, he worked at the local Ford dealership in his spare time. His father was a German immigrant who became a lamplighter on the streets of Saint Paul. Gerner saw the light when he quit school at age fifteen to become a plumber's apprentice. By age nineteen he realized he could make money playing baseball and began his career in Hensel, South Dakota, in 1916. He played for as little as fifteen dollars a game in places like Stillwater, Minnesota, and Whapeton and Hankinson in North Dakota. By 1920 he was making fifty dollars a game for Lamberton and Moose Lake in northern Minnesota. By 1925, bothered with chronic muscle spasms and fingers mangled by handling foul tips, he retired from baseball and spent the next thirty-three years in the auto parts business in Eau Claire. During that time Dutch watched generation after generation of pro baseball players come through the city on their way to the Major Leagues—or somewhere less glorious, like the auto parts business.

In the 1920s, with Babe Ruth hitting home runs at a record pace for the New York Yankees, baseball was popular in Eau Claire and across the nation. The first on-site radio broadcast of a baseball game took place in 1922 during the World Series. That same year in Eau Claire more than sixty thousand fans were watching heroes like Bullet Murphy, Babe Hurt, Bugs Mason, and Dutch Gerner. On game days a banner across Barstow Street, the main commercial thoroughfare, would proclaim "Baseball Today."

Eau Claire was roaring along in the 1920s. It had 20,960 people and at sixteen square miles it was geographically the third largest city in the state. The river city had 4,000 manufacturing jobs, 4,343 houses, 21 miles of paved streets (out of 100 miles of roads), 21 churches, 6 banks, 5 restaurants, 4 theaters, and 3 railroads. The city's skilled workers made paper, lumber, boxes, refrigerators, candy, overalls, sawmill machinery, gasoline engines, tractors, rubber tires, shoes, bedding, cigars, sausages, and beer.

One resident, Edwin Boberg, was so enamored with his lively hometown after the 1920s that he wrote a poem, "River Meets River," that said
in part,

> Where river meets river and friend meets friend,
> And over them both the heavens bend,
> Where the woods are green and the hills are fair
> And the air is cool—well, that's Eau Claire.

That was the idyllic view of Eau Claire if you were white. Most likely
blacks wouldn't have found the city so inviting. Like most northern
cities at the time, Eau Claire didn't openly discriminate against blacks or
promote segregation. Yet racism existed. For many years blacks weren't
allowed in the neighborhood where the Driving Park used to stand, under

Eau Claire's early pro baseball teams, like this one in 1922, were the forerunners of
the professional minor league teams that played in the city from 1933 through 1962.
(Photo courtesy of Chippewa Valley Museum, Eau Claire, Wisconsin)

a building covenant for the Woodland Homes Association. The eleventh item in the covenant, following such mundane items as landscaping, privies, and placement of structures, read: "The Lot or Lots hereby conveyed shall never be sold, transferred or leased to a colored person or persons." A search of the register of deeds at the Eau Claire County courthouse, where all property transactions dating back to the city's birth are filed, uncovered another such covenant. Dated 1915, it reads: "This lot is sold and deed given on the express covenant that no dwelling shall at any time be placed thereon of less than four rooms, shingle roofing, drop siding, painted and plastered or of brick, cement or stone, and that said premises shall never be occupied by a colored person or for any immoral use."

Why would people in historically white Eau Claire feel the need to protect themselves from blacks? In 1920, the city had just twenty-one black residents. Part of the irrational fear may have stemmed from their

northward migration during World War I, when many jobs opened in the industrialized North. From 1910 to 1930, one million blacks moved out of the South. Treatment of blacks was only beginning to change while Aaron grew up. Several Supreme Court rulings, beginning in the 1940s and extending through the Civil Rights Act of 1968, outlawed virtually all racial discrimination in the United States. Given the slow racial progress, it is not surprising that Aaron was apprehensive when he first saw his white teammates, his white coach, and all the other white residents of Eau Claire in 1952 and realized he was expected to trust and befriend them.

The spirit of civil rights was alive in Eau Claire, however. In 1932, two years before Aaron was born, a black baseball team from Detroit named the Gilkerson Union Giants played a game in Chippewa Falls against the semipro Eau Claire Cops. The Union Giants arrived by bus and slept at a fairgrounds in Chippewa Falls, making campfires to cook their food. It's not known if they couldn't find a hotel that would let them in or if they preferred to save money and rough it. In those days the winner of the game took 60 or 70 percent of the gate receipts and the loser received 30 or 40 percent. The Eau Claire Cops were leading 3–1 when the Union Giants came to bat for the last time. Eau Claire pitcher Art Johnson, a talented spitballer, uncharacteristically gave up three runs to lose the game. On the way home, someone asked him how the Union Giants got three runs off him. Johnson replied: "They've got to eat too."

Much of the groundwork for Aaron playing in Eau Claire was laid during the Depression. A new professional baseball team called the Bears— because it was affiliated with the Chicago Cubs, not the retreating stock market—was formed in Eau Claire in 1933. From 1933 until 1937, minor league games were played at Chappel Field, a skinned infield and burr-infested outfield on the flatlands about two miles upriver from the old Driving Park. The man behind the Bears was businessman Herman White. He served as president of the Bears, the Northern League, and the Wisconsin State League. Eventually he became one of only three members of baseball's minor league national executive committee, in effect giving the city a direct link to the latest baseball developments in the country. He was the man who was most responsible for keeping Eau Claire pro baseball alive for the next thirty years.

The first Bears team in 1933 drew more than three hundred players to a tryout. Many of them hiked or hitchhiked to the field. The coach from 1933 to 1937 was Johnny Mostil, a former All-Star major leaguer who played outfield for the Chicago White Sox. Mostil had the distinction of appearing in Ripley's "Believe It or Not" as the only Major League center fielder to catch a foul ball. In their first game the Bears lost 11–4 to East Grand Forks, Minnesota, to the disappointment of two thousand fans, many of whom avoided the forty-cent admission charge because the eight-foot-high board fences weren't yet finished. The first Bears finished 52-45. They survived midseason financial ruin once because good weather in Winnipeg, Canada, drew good crowds and permitted gate receipts sufficient to pay the bills and a second time when Eau Claire merchants guaranteed the players they would get paid if the Bears couldn't meet payroll.

For thirty summers, from 1933 through 1962, minor league professional baseball was Eau Claire's favorite pastime, drawing hundreds of thousands of fans. Eau Claire teams attracted the most fans in two of their pennant-winning seasons—103,150 in 1949 and 104,962 in 1951, an average of more than 1,600 a game. Of the city's twenty-seven Northern League teams (the league was inactive in the wartime years of 1943–45), two-thirds—eighteen—had winning seasons. Between 1942 and 1956 the Bears (known as the Braves starting in 1954) won five pennants, more than any other Northern League team.

The Bears' first pennant, in 1942, came with a record of 81–41, the best in city minor league history. The team featured future major leaguers Vic Johnson of Eau Claire and Clint Hartung of Texas. The owner of the team, Charlie Wachendorfer, was a well-to-do businessman who spared no expense with his players. He gave manager Rosy Ryan an open checkbook when the boys boarded their yellow school bus for road games. "We ate what we wanted to at restaurants, steaks most of the time," recalled former catcher Howie Bullock. Ryan was used to the star treatment: He had been a star pitcher for the New York Giants, winning thirty-three games in 1922 and 1923, the best years of his ten-year career. Ryan pitched in the 1922 and 1923 World Series, helping the Giants sweep Babe Ruth and the New York Yankees in 1922 before losing to the Yankees the next season.

Going to a baseball game became one of the city's most popular social activities. Knot Hole clubs encouraged kids to spend their summer afternoons and evenings at the park. Local businesses supported their Bears and filled the annual programs with their ads. The biggest employer in town,

United States Rubber Company, Gillette Tire Plant, took a full page to proclaim: "Science and Skill Count in Baseball; Science and Skill Count in Tires." The Electric Construction Company of Eau Claire encouraged residents to "Boost the Bears." Four dairies in the city reminded fans that Grade A milk and home runs are a great combination in Eau Claire. And fifty members of the Eau Claire Tavern League wished the Bears good luck in a full-page ad. It was that way around the country. "There was one period after World War II when every town big enough to have a bank also had a professional baseball team, and the peak of excitement was reached when the bank was robbed or the baseball team won a pennant," Atlanta journalist Furman Bisher once wrote.

Milk and baseball were often part of a marketing plan to get fans to the stadium. For example, a game on June 24, 1958, between the Eau Claire Braves and the Mallards of Minot, North Dakota, was billed as "Dairy Day at Carson Park." The team announced to fans that "ice cream bars and other dairy products will be given to fans. Four newly chosen Alice in Dairyland princesses will be on hand to add to the festivities, and an added attraction will be a milking contest. After the game there will be dancing under the stars at the park."

At neighborhood watering holes, like Ray's Place, Mooney's Bar, Adler's, or the Last Chance, middle-aged fans converged after the games and talked about the hometown team under neon signs for Walter's Beer, a German lager produced since 1889 about two miles from the stadium. As with the Bears and Braves, Walter's Beer isn't around anymore.

Carson Park became a second home for many residents during the summer. It was Eau Claire's front yard. "That was the big time," recalled city resident Bill Anderson, who grew up in Eau Claire and was a Bears volunteer during his teens. "It was such a big part of the summer for any kid. If you didn't go to the movies you'd go to the ball game. There were fifteen hundred people a night. It was amazing. There were only thirty-five thousand people in town."

Eau Claire has never been a hotbed for sending homegrown players to the majors, although two players did make their mark. Vic Johnson grew up in Eau Claire and was excited when he made the 1942 Bears and started earning the ninety-dollars-a-month salary. Two years later he broke into the majors with the Boston Red Sox. His career wasn't a long one; he went back to the minors in 1947 and played until 1949 when he got tired of the traveling. Then he jumped at a job offer as the director of a physical education program at the YMCA in Eau Claire. He was proud to have reached the majors, and his career provided one memory that stood out among many. In 1945 he and the Red Sox shut out the Joe DiMaggio–led New York Yankees at Yankee Stadium, enough of an achievement to make him a celebrity of sorts in his hometown for the rest of his life. In 1998, the local newspaper featured Johnson in a "sports flashback" column that included a color photo of him in his Boston uniform under the heading "Game Boy." He actually threw sixteen consecutive innings of shutout ball that year against the mighty Yankees. Despite a 6-4 record in 1945 Johnson was traded to Cleveland in the off-season and spent part of 1946 on the Indians' pitching staff with Bob Feller before winding up in the minors later that year. But he never forgot the sixteen innings when the mighty men in pinstripes couldn't get a run off him.

Along with Johnson, Tom Poquette made the jump from Eau Claire sandlots to the majors in the 1970s, playing seven years with the Kansas City Royals and Boston Red Sox. He hit a high of .302 in 1976 in his best full season, when he made the majors' All-Rookie team. Injuries finally pushed him from the game in 1982. A smooth-swinging lefty, he returned to coach in the Royals' farm system in 1988 and became the Major League team's batting coach in 1997.

One player who grew up near Eau Claire and debuted with the Bears became a star in the majors. In 1940 the Bears signed Andy Pafko, the son of Czechoslovakian immigrants who lived on a dairy farm in Boyceville forty miles west of Eau Claire. A high school athletic star, Pafko tried out for the Class D Eau Claire Bears but was told by manager Ivy Griffin to come back in a year. He went home to work on the farm, thought the dream was over, and played softball once a week. In August, however, Griffin was short of outfielders and drove to Boyceville to get Pafko. "It was harvest time, and I was putting up the straw," Pafko said. "I saw this big car drive in the driveway. It was the manager of the Eau Claire team, and he said, 'You come along with me.' I couldn't get off that stack fast enough, take a shower, and get in the car with him."

Pafko hit only .209 in twenty games with Eau Claire, but the next year at Class D Green Bay of the Wisconsin State League he hit .349. Then it was on to Macon, Georgia, of the South Atlantic League (Class B), where he hit .300, and Los Angeles of the Pacific Coast League (AAA) in 1943.

He led the Pacific Coast League in hitting (.356), hits (215), and RBIs (118). The Chicago Cubs had seen enough. They called up the hustling twenty-one-year-old that fall.

Pafko got a single and double in his first two Major League at bats, driving in four runs in the process, and was on his way to a celebrated career. In 1945 he played center field and helped the Cubs win their last pennant of the century. In 1947 he started in center field for the National League in the All-Star Game. The starter in center for the American League was his idol, Joe DiMaggio.

Pafko was traded to the Brooklyn Dodgers in 1951. He was there less than two seasons but long enough to play with Jackie Robinson and the gang. And long enough to watch Bobby Thomson's "shot heard 'round the world" go over his head in left field as the Giants won the 1951 pennant. He was in the World Series with the Dodgers in 1952, part of what is considered the team's best outfield ever—Pafko in left, Duke Snider in center, and Carl Furillo in right. In *Boys of Summer*, Roger Kahn's classic book about the early 1950s Dodgers, Pafko even merited his own chapter, "The Sandwich Man." Pafko didn't consider himself in the same class with the Dodger greats but saw himself as a sandwich on the lineup with a bunch of steaks. Yet the unassuming Pafko was chosen to the Brooklyn Dodgers' Hall of Fame in 1994.

Andy Pafko started his long pro baseball career with the Eau Claire Bears in 1940, broke into the majors with the Chicago Cubs, and later played with Henry Aaron on the Milwaukee Braves teams of the late 1950s.

(Photo courtesy of the *Eau Claire Leader-Telegram*)

When Pafko was traded to Milwaukee he was thrilled to return to Wisconsin. He helped the Braves open County Stadium and win the 1957 World Series before he retired after the 1959 season to become a Braves coach. Oddly enough, he became roommates with Thomson when he was traded to the Braves. And in 1954, when Thomson broke his ankle in spring training and the Braves needed a new outfielder, Henry Aaron was put into the starting lineup. An opening day picture in 1954 shows all the Braves lined up in the dugout. Three of them had been Eau Claire Bears: Pafko, Aaron, and Billy Bruton.

Pafko had a .285 career batting average, and the folks in Boyceville—who would listen to his World Series games on a radio in the high school gymnasium—couldn't have been more proud. He played in four World Series and four All-Star games. Boyceville dedicated an athletic park in his name on May 24, 1986, and the governor's office proclaimed Andy Pafko Day in Wisconsin. It's Andy Pafko Day every day when he returns to Boyceville from his Chicago-area home. He signs autographs for kids and adults every time he goes back to visit his brothers, their parents' graves, and the old farm where it all began one day when he was putting up the straw.

Pafko's top salary with the Braves was $35,000 a year, but he loved the game so much he said he would have played for nothing. "You did," his wife, Ellen, often told him. If only Pafko had saved the baseball cards of himself, he would have been handsomely compensated. In 1998 a Topps card of Pafko in his Brooklyn uniform sold for $83,870 at a sports memorabilia auction. The card drew the second highest bid of 1,388 items in the $2.6 million auction held by Mastro Fine Sports of Chicago. Only Lou Gehrig's Yankees home jersey sold for more: $108,425. A baseball signed by Henry Aaron, Babe Ruth, and Roger Maris fetched only $5,909. The price paid for the Pafko card was surprising considering he isn't a Hall of Fame member. But the card came out of a previously unopened pack, was in mint condition, and was (for no apparent reason) the number one card in the set. The year of the card, 1952, was the year of Topps's first full card sets. Pafko celebrated his eightieth birthday in 2001, and a few months later a reprint of the 1952 card was given to the first thirty thousand fans at the Cubs' home game on August 21 against the Brewers.

Watching Henry Aaron make it to the big leagues wasn't an anomaly for Eau Claire baseball fans. Between 1950 and 1961 Bears fans saw sixteen of

their minor leaguers advance to the majors, more than any other Northern League team. Some of them became pretty fair major leaguers: Billy
Bruton (1950 Bears), Johnny Goryl (1952, 1954), Manny Jimenez (1958),
Lee Maye (1955), Ron Piche (1956), Rico Carty (1961), Tony Cloninger
(1958), Wes Covington (1952), and Joe Torre (1960). Carty led the National
League in hitting in 1970 with a .366 average and averaged .299 during a
fifteen-year career.

In addition, the younger brother of a famous Brave, Tommie Aaron,
played in Eau Claire in 1958 and 1959. He hit twenty-six homers for Eau
Claire in 1959 and looked as if he would be a better home run hitter
than his brother. Tommie and Henry wound up as roommates with the
Braves in the 1960s, but Tommie's career was over before Henry hit his
600th home run.

The Eau Claire influence, like that of most successful minor league
operations, could be traced throughout baseball: Players, umpires, coaches,
and front-office personnel throughout the league had come through Eau

Tommie Aaron followed in his
older brother's footsteps when
he played for the Eau Claire Braves
in 1958.
(Photo courtesy of the
Eau Claire Leader-Telegram)

Claire. In 1964 three of the four top National League hitters were Milwaukee Braves and former Eau Claire stars. Carty, a rookie, hit .330, Aaron hit .328, and Torre hit .321. The only one better was Roberto Clemente at .339.

Prior to 1950, Major League regulars such as Jim Delsing (1946 Bears), Hank Majeski (1936), Chuck Tanner (1947–48), Pafko (1940), Wes Westrum (1941), Phil Masi (1938), and Stan Spence (1936) starred in Eau Claire. After nine seasons in the minor leagues, Tanner broke into the majors as Henry Aaron's teammate on the 1955 Milwaukee Braves. Tanner became a successful manager from 1970 to 1988; his Pittsburgh Pirates won the 1979 World Series behind Willie Stargell. Dave Garcia played for the 1941 Bears and never played in the majors, but he managed the California Angels and Cleveland Indians between 1977 and 1982.

Fans also saw the stars of the visiting teams and soon-to-be Major League stars: Mateo Alou, Steve Barber, Lou Brock, Camilo Carreon, Orlando Cepeda, Donn Clendenon, Roger Maris, Joe Pepitone, Vada Pinson, Don Elston, Jim "Mudcat" Grant, Bob Turley, Tito Francona, Don Mincher, Ray Sadecki, Don Larsen, Gaylord Perry, and Jim Perry. Larsen played for the Aberdeen Pheasants in 1947 and 1948, and on October 8, 1956, as a New York Yankee he pitched the first perfect game in World Series history. Cepeda played for the Saint Cloud Rox in 1956, was National League Rookie of the Year in 1958 (when he hit the first Major League home run ever on the West Coast for the San Francisco Giants), and played through 1974. He was inducted into the Hall of Fame in 1999. Brock played for Saint Cloud in 1961 and later set the Major League record for stolen bases for a season (118 in 1974) and for a career. Brock and Gaylord Perry are also in the Hall of Fame.

Eau Claire even got credit for putting Braves knuckleball pitcher Phil Niekro on the road to the Hall of Fame. During his acceptance speech on the steps of the Hall of Fame in Cooperstown, the same place where Burleigh Grimes and Aaron had stood, Niekro mentioned that his career started in Eau Claire. Later, however, he acknowledged that it didn't start there. In his first contract in 1959 he was assigned to Eau Claire, but after spring training he was sent instead to the Pony League in Wellsville, New York. He had heard from Braves players at training camp in Waycross, Georgia, that Eau Claire was a great place to play. "I was always disappointed I never got to go there," he said later.

One of the highlights in the history of minor league baseball in Eau Claire was the 1951 Northern League All-Star Game at Carson Park. The game featured the top players from the league versus the Bears, who were the host team because they were in first place on July 4. The July 17 night game drew the largest crowd in Carson Park history, 4,368, or about 12 percent of Eau Claire's population. It was standing room only, and the Bears didn't disappoint their fans. George Sentementes drove home outfielder Horace Garner, an All-Star selection, with the winning run in the bottom of the ninth as the Bears won, 7–6.

AFTER HENRY

The name of the Eau Claire team changed from the Bears to the Braves in 1954 to reflect the parent club, the Boston Braves, which had moved to Milwaukee in 1953. It remained the Eau Claire Braves until 1962, its final season, when the team was forced to quit operating because attendance was low and advertising revenue had dried up. Attendance dropped from 38,000 in 1959 to 36,000 in 1960 and 26,000 in 1961 (only about 400 per game). The stage was set for one last season in 1962, and attendance got worse: 20,906, or only 331 per game, the worst in the Northern League that year and the worst in team history.

Suddenly, the team that had captured the spirit of the city in the 1940s and 1950s was in a no-win financial situation. The Eau Claire Braves had to start counting pennies. In 1961 they published a "Do You Know" financial fact sheet, telling the public that the previous season they had spent $2,469.74 on baseballs and $615 on bats. The player salaries totaled $23,431.20, but the Milwaukee Braves paid $9,100 of that. The Eau Claire Braves figured that if they explained how much it actually cost to operate a pro baseball team, the fans might get the picture that their support was critical to the team's survival.

The team didn't go down in 1962 without an appeal from team officials, who pleaded for help in the *Telegram* in late August. They had an ally in the paper's sports editor, Clell Buzzell, who then was the team vice president. A sports page story headed "EC Braves Face Money Crisis, Seek Help of Fans to Continue" reported that the Braves were the number one seasonal industry in the city, drawing people from more than seventy-two cities each summer, including scouts and officials from all Major League teams. Much of the team's annual budget of sixty thousand dollars went back into the community's economy. But the team was struggling mightily to remain solvent. In fact, the Braves said that if they didn't get a thousand paid admissions for each game of a three-game home stand against Duluth-Superior, the team may not finish the season. The plea, which was released by team president George "Pappy" Wojahn, stated: "This deficit has reached the point where the average attendance this year cannot hope to pull the operation out of the red in the remaining nine home dates. The Braves are on an unsound financial footing with both of the banks with which they are now doing business. We owe large sums to the local creditors, who it must be said have been most understanding. We feel that it is our right to ask the people of Eau Claire, and in particular our civic leaders, to try and help us save this proven contributing industry for our community." The Braves appealed to baseball fans who were traveling to games elsewhere. "We are asking those of you who are buying your baseball out of town, whether it be in Milwaukee or in Minneapolis, to try your home town product at least once during these last nine days of the 1962 season."

The team didn't report attendance in the final box scores, but whatever the figures were they at least got the Braves through the end of the season. In their final regular season home games on August 31, 1962, the Braves swept a doubleheader from Winnipeg.

The Braves didn't leave Eau Claire without one last hurrah. Under manager Jim Fanning, who would leave the front office and return to the field briefly in the 1980s as manager of the Montreal Expos, the Braves won fifteen of their last nineteen games to finish third in the pennant race and make the Northern League playoffs. Their final home game ever was a 2–1 win over Grand Forks, in a one-game midweek playoff on September 4, 1962. Then in the final series they swept a best-of-three playoff in Aberdeen against the Pheasants, the team that had won the pennant. The playoff championship was Eau Claire's first since 1941 and only the third in club history. In the 1940s or 1950s an achievement like that would have reverberated around Eau Claire and received top billing in the sports pages, if not some mention on the front page. With its sagging attendance, however, minor league baseball was no longer the darling of the local media. The news of the Eau Claire Braves' championship in 1962 ran on the bottom of the second page of the *Telegram*'s sports section under the headline "Braves Slug Out 14–6 win, Take Polar Playoff Crown." High school football dominated the front page of sports, and the Braves' triumph ran even below a photo promoting the Eau Claire Archers annual Broadhead Shoot that weekend.

About two months after the season ended, club chairman Randall "Ran" Bezanson broke the news that the team most likely would not return for 1963. From 1959 to 1961 the club was at about the break-even point financially, but Bezanson told the *Milwaukee Journal* that in 1962 it lost $9,264. The Milwaukee Braves promised to pay part of the debt, but it wasn't enough. The only solution was for the Milwaukee Braves to buy the Eau Claire Braves, and they refused. Eau Claire had been in the Braves' minor league system longer than any other team, and the city was the only one to have a team in the Northern League every year since its inception in 1933.

Was it coincidence that the Eau Claire Braves failed in 1962, one year after the debut of the Minnesota Twins? Suddenly, Major League baseball was just two hours away by car, and the Milwaukee Braves were less than five hours away. Distances now seemed shorter as cars became more reliable and comfortable and the highway system improved. Before 1953 the closest Major League team to Eau Claire was in Chicago.

The problem wasn't just in Eau Claire. Of the eight teams in the Northern League in 1962, seven lost money, between six thousand and twelve thousand dollars per team. Attendance fell in the league from 647,000 in 1949 to 207,000 in 1961, a 68 percent drop. The story was similar in minor leagues across the country, from a high of 42 million fans in 1949 to 10 million in 1963, a drop of 76 percent. During that span, the number of leagues fell from fifty-nine to eighteen and the number of teams from 461 to 147.

Forces inside and outside of baseball killed the Northern League. The Eau Claire Braves complained that the distant location of two new teams, Bismarck and Minot in North Dakota, greatly increased travel expenses. Bezanson said the change that put Eau Claire over the edge was the loss of its radio broadcasts. "Prior to 1960 we always sold our broadcasts. After that we couldn't give them away. Local stations started carrying the Braves' games, and the Minnesota Twins' games as well. We just got squeezed out," Bezanson said.

Some say television kept fans from the ballpark. Almost every home had a television set, and suddenly fans could see Major League baseball without leaving their living rooms to watch an inferior band of players, the minor leaguers. Some blamed the minor leagues' demise on the ever-expanding number of Major League teams that raided their farm clubs of talent and didn't give them proper financial support. After Eau Claire folded in 1962 the entire Northern League nearly went under in 1964, but it was resurrected as a rookie league and struggled on until 1971.

The Bears and Braves had been the social spirit of the community for thirty years, but Eau Claire's minor league days were now part of a by-gone era. Baseball as the main spectator sport in Eau Claire began and ended about the same time as passenger train service to the city. The first passenger train came in 1870, about three years after the first recorded base-ball game. The last passenger train, the Twin Cities "400" on the Chicago and North Western Railway, passed through the city in July 1963, ten months after the last minor league baseball game. Neither has returned.

Attempts to start a new minor league team in Eau Claire failed in the 1970s, 1980s, and 1990s. As salaries rose in the majors, so did the cost of fielding a minor league team. When teams found out that Eau Claire wouldn't agree to money-making improvements at their old park, they quietly withdrew their proposals. Despite their fond memories of the minor league glory days, city residents seemed content to let them pass. They weren't willing to court another team, call it their own, and then have it split town, as so many pro sports franchises were wont to do dur-ing those years. The Braves left Boston and Milwaukee. The Dodgers left Brooklyn, and the Giants left New York for the West Coast. The Senators left Washington. The Pilots left Seattle for Milwaukee. Disenfranchise-ment was caused by more than athletic teams moving. Assassins struck down two Kennedys, Martin Luther King Jr., and John Lennon. Nixon resigned the presidency. Young men didn't come home from Vietnam. Hostages spent 444 days in Iran. The *Challenger* blew up. The people of Eau Claire, as elsewhere, were scarred when something important was taken away. Eau Claire had its run, they figured. Baseball wasn't the same game in the 1980s or 1990s as it was before and after World War II, when it was considered the only game. Professional baseball was over in Eau Claire, at least for the century.

After a nine-year respite, baseball as a spectator sport was reborn at Carson Park, although in a much subdued form. The semipro Eau Claire

Cavaliers debuted June 6, 1971, and over the past thirty-plus years have fielded some of the top amateur teams in the country. Five times they won the unlimited age Continental Amateur Baseball Association (CABA) World Series.

The Cavs have won all of their world titles at Carson Park, in 1994–97 and 2001 (the latter when the Long Island Storm had to forfeit the championship game to catch their flight back east). The Cavs' titles came under coach Harvey Tomter, who racked up nearly fourteen hundred victories with the team. A local athletic star, Tomter had played for an amateur team at Carson Park in the early 1950s on days when the Bears didn't play. Tomter even played one game with the 1952 Bears and Henry Aaron, joining them for an exhibition in La Crosse just before the Northern League playoffs. Under Tomter and another coach, the Cavs have never had a losing season, but spectator-wise have never caught on in a city that is used to a higher caliber of ball. The crowds typically number two hundred or smaller, unless it's a promotional night when numerous prizes are given away.

The Cavaliers are a mix of college players and ex-college players who still have a little something left in their arms and bats. The Cavs play most of their games at home, many of them against cities that are hard to find on the map, such as Miesville, Minnesota, or against a group of ex-high school players, Cavs wannabes, who named themselves the Eau Claire Bears. The games are often lopsided in the Cavs' favor. Often, the few fans are family members or aging men who remember the Bears and wax nostalgic at the thought of a beer, a hot dog, and a baseball game on a mild summer evening.

Continuing in the Eau Claire tradition, several Cavs have advanced to the Major Leagues. One of them was Kerry Ligtenberg, although he pitched in just one game for the Cavs en route to the majors with the Atlanta Braves. In 1998 Ligtenberg was the winning pitcher in relief when the Braves beat the Milwaukee Brewers in Atlanta to mark Milwaukee's return to the National League. It was one more chance—albeit nebulous—for Eau Claire to say it still was sending minor leaguers to the Braves. As of 2001, the Cavs (thirty-one years) had officially outlasted minor league baseball (thirty years) in Eau Claire.

The Cavs aren't the only Carson Park tenant. In the 1990s as many as two hundred games per year were played at Carson Park, sometimes four a day by the Cavs, the Bears, and a teenage American Legion team sponsored by the owner of a local pizza franchise. At one Legion game, fewer than fifty people dotted the bleachers on a perfect summer night. An occasional yell echoing off the grandstand sounded more like a voice from a root cellar. It certainly wasn't an echo of the past, when fans often filled the park.

In 1997 the stadium was renovated extensively for the first time since it was built. A community fundraising effort helped provide the $750,000 needed for new seating, concession stands, rest rooms, a press box, a plaza around the Aaron statue, and cosmetic improvements—a new sign, wrought-iron railings, and pennant flags waving from the rooftop. When it was all spruced up, the park not only was functional again but retained its historic feel. The community consensus was that the stadium needed to be preserved because it still was structurally sound. Since Eau Claire is filled with pragmatic Midwestern bargain hunters, many of them the sons and daughters of frugal northern European farmers whose names end in -son—Pederson, Larson, Nelson—there was absolutely no talk of building a new stadium that would boost property tax bills. Of course, with no minor league team, they didn't need a new stadium. After it was remodeled, however, some people began to wonder if such a nice old stadium was being effectively utilized when less than 10 percent of the thirty-five hundred seats were filled on most nights.

Many residents truly were in love with the idea that Carson Park, sixty years old, had become more than a stadium. Without question, they agreed, it should be preserved. It was more of a hallowed place to them than the regional history museum that stands beyond center field in the park. The stadium was where history actually happened and where they saw it happen. It was a symbol of the city's past and present, the place where old-timers who were retired from the local tire factory, paper mill, or brewery could reminisce about the time they saw skinny Henry Aaron hit a home run, pudgy Joe Torre throw out a runner, or muscular Roger Maris slap a double. It's the place where seventeen-year-old high school and American Legion players could hear the long-ago tales from veteran coaches and wonder if they too had the talent that would take them just as far in the game.

The stadium renovation made Bill Anderson proud. The Eau Claire boy who chased down foul balls during the late 1940s and early 1950s went

The statue of Henry Aaron is the centerpiece of a pedestrian plaza outside
Carson Park baseball stadium, which was remodeled in the 1990s.

(Dan Reiland photo, courtesy of the *Eau Claire Leader-Telegram*)

away to Minneapolis to become an architect, became a fastpitch softball player, and followed with a passion pro baseball and the career of Aaron. He returned to Eau Claire with a passion to keep his hometown the way it was when he was growing up. It was a place where we "never locked our doors. You expected everything to be perfect and basically it was. There were no killings. The worst thing was if a neighbor came home drunk and was driving on the rims of his wheels." Two years after the Aaron statue went up, Anderson was hired as the architect for the stadium renovation. He probably would have done it for nothing. He liked seeing it look young again and realized that it now would last another sixty years, longer than he would. Carson Park stadium mirrors Anderson's life: It opened the year he was born in Eau Claire.

The stadium, one of many built during the Depression by the WPA (another was Wade Stadium in Duluth in 1941), has changed very little, a testament to the fact it is in a small city where there has been no pressure for better facilities. All that remains now of Metropolitan Stadium in Bloomington, Minnesota—where Harmon Killebrew hit his 500th home run on August 10, 1971, and Rod Carew stroked many of his three-thousand-plus hits—is the home plate. The Mall of America now stands on the site, but the mall builders marked home plate as the new steel girders rose around it. The Met's home plate now is near Camp Snoopy, and when you look up, as Killebrew used to when his thirty-three-ounce, thirty-five-inch bat had just flattened a baseball, the sky is no longer the limit: It's sky lights, steel support beams, and the curving tracks of a roller coaster. You have to go indoors to see the Met's home plate now—just like the Minnesota Twins' home plate in the downtown Minneapolis Metrodome. The Met was built in 1956 and torn down in 1981. Shopping has been great, but baseball in Minnesota never has been the same. The Twins were beginning to realize their mistake as they tried to drum up support for a new outdoor stadium at the start of the century. Worse yet, early in 2002 the Twins weren't even sure they would field a team. Major League Baseball was considering eliminating two Major League teams for financial reasons. The Twins were one of them, although they did play in 2002.

At Carson Park, baseball is played straight up. A ten-foot-high chain-link fence, covered by a blue tarp, surrounds the outfield. With no minor league team revenues to worry about, no investors to appease, and no

salaries to pay, there is no need to plaster the outfield walls with advertising boards for cellular phones, specialty beers, ISPs, HMOs, SUVs, or
any other sign of the times. With no infusion of marketing money from
a privately owned team, Carson Park has avoided the age of Baseball as
Sideshow. There are no dressed-up animal mascots, ball girls in hot pants,
and fan tricks between innings, no air guns loaded on the back of pickup
trucks that roam the sidelines between innings and shoot wadded-up
T-shirts into the crowd, no disc jockeys who spin Frisbees into the stands
on Cool 96.8 Night.

For the most part, anyway. The largest annual crowd at Carson Park is
a free-for-all sponsored by a local tire company. If you want to attract a
crowd of Americans, the people on earth with the most stuff, promise them
more free stuff. Even if they go home with a CD of some country music
star that they've never heard of, they're happy. Tire Night lets everyone in
free and gives away prizes between every at bat. Whether it's a good game
or not, most of the three thousand people hang around until the later innings to see who will win the bicycle or the other grand prize of the night.
They consume large quantities of Leinenkugel's beer, soda, popcorn, hot
dogs, and nachos and cheese, stop to read the plaques on the Henry Aaron
statue to their kids, say to themselves, "What better way to spend a summer evening than at the ballpark?" and are pleased they don't have to drive
home from Minneapolis or Milwaukee after seeing a baseball game.

One of the other big nights is the Fourth of July, when the Cavs always
play a twilight doubleheader and fans fill the baseball stadium, football
stadium, and the wooded park in anticipation of the city fireworks show
at dusk. On a recent Fourth, driving through the park in late afternoon,
I saw fans heading to the baseball game, children riding the minirailroad
across the street, families picnicking in the woods, people fishing and
playing volleyball, more families taking part in the Old-Fashioned Fourth
at the nearby museum, and a man singing Billy Joel's "Piano Man" in a
monotone to a small audience during a karaoke contest near the rest
rooms. His amplified, off-key rendition could be heard throughout the
park, but no one seemed to mind.

For most of the 1990s, the only side attraction to Carson Park baseball was watching wiry, middle-aged Billy, a Forrest Gump of Eau Claire,
mingle with fans while taking calls on a two-way radio and sprinting
with Gump-type speed (usually outrunning preteen boys) through the

concourse and out into the parking lot for foul balls, all to save the team a few dollars. Billy lives in a group home, and Carson Park is his home away from home in the summer. He patrols the stadium in a uniformlike jump suit as though it is his backyard. The fair-weather fans throw him odd glances, the regulars leave him alone, and his friends make him feel at home. Billy became immortal among ball boys when he chased a ball thief all the way out of the park to a Dairy Queen a mile away. He got the ball. Then he ran a mile back to show it off and turn it in to team officials.

Other than the entertainment provided by Billy, it's no-frills baseball mostly. They still play baseball in Eau Claire the way they did in 1937. Because the park sits on top of a bluff, city residents can tell if an evening game is on simply by looking for the lights or listening for the public address announcer, whose statements carry over the water and into the lower west side neighborhood like a voice from the heavens. *"After five innings ..., it's the Cavaliers eight ... and Roseville one."* People just out for a drive through the park at 9 P.M. can see megawatt halos illumi-nating white figures in the dew moving to the sounds of leather, wood, and wind in thick grass between chalk lines under an orange-sliced sky, a nightly dance of inspiration, perspiration, and hope staged by young, athletic men. For those in uniform, baseball in Eau Claire has always meant living a bit of the Major League dream, the chance to play in front of a paying crowd on a field with Major League dimensions.

Every summer Carson Park's World Series, the CABA, draws teams from coast to coast. It's more an invitational than a true tournament, more a true test of which teams can raise the money to attend than which teams are deserving to play. None of the teams have to qualify. Some of the players have pot bellies and are in their forties. Some of them are buffed young prospects who have that hungry look in their eye and could make the Major Leagues someday.

Before an evening game in the 1998 series, the California Colt 45's took turns photographing each other leaning on the Henry Aaron statue. They may have been too tired to stand on their own. The young men, mostly college players trying to improve their games in the summer, each had sold two hundred dollars worth of T-shirts in Whittier, California, to finance the trip, then piled into four vans and drove forty hours straight to reach Eau Claire, leaving at 11 P.M. Saturday night and arriving Monday afternoon. One of their players seemed destined for the majors on the basis of his name alone. He was a shortstop named Ozzie—Ozzie Madera. "We couldn't wait to get to Wisconsin. We had heard about Carson Park. Everybody was excited to see Hank Aaron," Madera said.

Other teams came from Marlboro, New Jersey; Blue Springs, Missouri; Chicago, Elmhurst, Melrose Park, and Lombard, Illinois; and White Bear Lake, Minnesota. The East Coast was represented by a team from Brooklyn, which was sponsored by a food wholesaler, a sports store, and the Thurman Munson Foundation, named after the late New York Yankee catcher. The Brooklyn players, mostly ex-minor leaguers and college players in their early twenties, were 40-12 in the Staten Island Baseball Federation before coming to Eau Claire, where they didn't advance to the winner's bracket and were hanging out one last day at a local hotel before heading home. Many of the players also doubled in the Pedrin Zorilla Spanish League, also called the Last Chance League, according to captain Melvin Martinez. During Major League Baseball's strike year in 1994, the Last Chance League sent seventeen scabs to the majors, said Martinez as he dressed in the hotel room he shared with a dark-haired girlfriend and which served as the revolving-door headquarters for the team. Martinez, a high school coach and special education teacher, said Brooklyn still misses its Dodgers. All that's left, he laments, is a sign "Ebbets Field Was Here," which hangs on fifty-story housing projects and a new expressway named after Jackie Robinson, who's "still a hero."

The elder statesman for Brooklyn was thin, Gumbylike pitcher Terric McFarlin, age thirty, who saw his Major League dreams fizzle in the early 1990s. He's now president of his own business, Mid-City Electrical Corporation in Whitestone, New York, and plays amateur ball simply for his love of the game. It was his third straight season traveling halfway across the country to play in Eau Claire. His teammates revered him as an ex–major leaguer, although he actually wasn't. "He made the Show," they said with the swagger that young people use when they are near what they dream of—celebrity. They said he once hung out with Ken Griffey Jr.

He did. Once. McFarlin grew up in Brooklyn and went to Lafayette High, which produced big league pitchers Johnny Franco and Frank Viola. McFarlin started pitching at age thirteen and was playing semipro ball at age twenty-one when a Dodgers scout signed him and sent him to an instructional league. Soon he was in Class A ball in Bakersfield, California, and earned the nickname Robo because his right arm never seemed to tire. He breezed through Classes A, AA, and AAA and in 1995 went to spring training with the Seattle Mariners. Then he was mysteriously released without any appearances that spring and couldn't catch on with another team, believing that he had been blackballed for crossing the picket line during the players strike. "I wish it turned out differently. I was actually enjoying it, the fans, the autograph sessions, the meetings. Now I don't get to do anything like that," McFarlin said.

Minutes earlier he had been in the parking lot of the Eau Claire Ramada Inn instructing teammates who were working on their curve balls. It seemed a mighty long way from spring training with the Mariners and Junior to a workout at a blacktop hotel parking lot in Eau Claire. "Now I play ball when I can with the teams I'm comfortable with," McFarlin said, citing an 18–1 record in 1998 and a 45–3 career record since Seattle released him. "My baseball career as a professional is shot. As far as me playing the game, I'll play until I'm forty. I love the game. I'm certainly glad there's baseball. It's beautiful. It's beautiful. I don't care if there's only one fan in the stands. I'd pitch. Baseball is the best thing that ever happened to me."

McFarlin, who wore a thick gold chain that looped through a gold baseball pin, said the Henry Aaron statue at Carson Park stadium didn't mean that much to him. Things of the past don't, he said. Even if he and Aaron were black men who had something in common, a love for baseball. Even if Aaron was once refused service at a restaurant in Eau Claire in 1952, and even if, according to teammates, Pop Wallace, a black member of McFarlin's Brooklyn team, suffered the same humiliation in Eau Claire in 1996. Even if Henry Aaron was called every derogatory name known to Americans as he closed in on Ruth's home run record in 1974, and even if McFarlin remembers once being called boy in Eau Claire. Even if McFarlin resembles the young Henry Aaron depicted on the statue. "My teammates looked at the statue and said, 'You look like him.' I'm not happy or thrilled. Being black in my eyes is no different. I try not to think too much about all that stuff." McFarlin believes that, no matter what color you are, "leave a good impression." When Aaron played in Eau Claire, he often stopped to talk to a black man who could be found hanging out on a street corner. Aaron has always remembered the advice the man gave him. "You come here to play baseball. Then play baseball and do your best. Remember, it's the impression that you leave."

In 1952 one of the top pitchers for the Eau Claire Bears was a young lefthander named Bobby Brown. He too was from Brooklyn. It's doubtful that either Brown or McFarlin knew they were extending a long baseball association between Eau Claire and Brooklyn. Burleigh Grimes, who started his career in Eau Claire in 1912, helped make the Brooklyn Dodgers famous in the 1920s. Andy Pafko, who started his career in Eau Claire in 1940, helped make Brooklyn infamous in 1951 when he stood at the base of the left field wall at Ebbets Field and watched Bobby Thomson's ninth-inning home run sail into history to give the Giants the pennant. Pafko was back in a Brooklyn uniform the next year when the Dodgers lost four games to three to the New York Yankees in the World Series.

One of the Dodgers faithful who felt the sting of Thomson's home run in 1951 was an eleven-year-old boy living on Avenue T in Brooklyn, Joseph Paul Torre. Five years later, Torre would be working out at Ebbets Field, and in 1960 he would have something in common with Grimes, Pafko, Bobby Brown, and a yet-to-be-born Terric McFarlin—he too was playing baseball in Eau Claire.

chapter 3

ON THE ROAD IN THE
NORTHERN LEAGUE

When Henry Aaron, Joe Torre, and legions of other Eau Claire minor leaguers weren't playing at Carson Park, they were crisscrossing northern Wisconsin, Minnesota, North Dakota, South Dakota, and even parts of Canada—the parts with roads—to play in the Northern League's other ballparks. The scenery might have been pretty in places, but the routine of packing up equipment, driving hundreds of miles in summer heat while sandwiched into an un-air-conditioned vehicle, then hopping out to play baseball in some Midwestern outpost even farther north or west than "Eau Where?" was the most forgettable part of being a minor leaguer. Easily. Or the most romantic, depending on your sense of humor. Torre, used to the bright lights of Brooklyn and New York, remembers warming up for games at some of the rickety, wooden Northern League ballparks and wondering when the groundskeepers would turn on the lights. They were on, teammates would tell him.

Teams could take fourteen players on the road and sometimes an umpire, meaning one player was the odd man out, or, considering the cramped conditions, the lucky man out. Behind one of the cars was a two-wheel trailer with all the equipment. The cars were so burdened that the team sent four extra tires to make sure the players would get back. The roads were mostly gravel and shaky and dusty enough to rattle off the hubcaps, make sleeping difficult, and dislodge any intestinal blockage incurred from a succession of roast beef and mashed potato dinners at roadside cafés.

In 1952 Aaron and the Bears touched bases in ballparks as far away as Sioux Falls, South Dakota, near the Iowa border, Aberdeen, South Dakota, near the North Dakota border, and Grand Forks, North Dakota. In Grand Forks Aaron was about as far north as one could get in the lower forty-eight states—a long, long way from Mobile in terms of miles but especially of culture. Lefse, bratwurst, waving wheat and corn fields, pine-fringed freshwater lakes, dairy farms, ski-jumping towers on the horizons, Paul Bunyan folklore, and blond, blue-eyed, freckled, sunburned, innocent-looking Scandinavians. It wasn't anything like the region where he grew up with its soul food, cotton fields, salt water, shipyards, paper mills, and black skin, the urban, segregated Gulf Coast city of Mobile with the shadowy history of the Ku Klux Klan and the Confederacy lurking behind the white folks he seldom came in contact with.

For road trips the 1952 Bears piled into two nine-passenger 1949 Chrysler airport limousines plastered with Bears logos. The cars were hand-me-downs; they had been used the year before with the Braves' Class A farm team in Hartford, Connecticut, in the Eastern League, so they had plenty of miles on them. Elmer Toth and Julie Bowers knew the cars well because they rode in them in 1951 while playing for Hartford. All the team equipment weaved behind the Chryslers as they headed out across the Mississippi River to the Minnesota prairies or up north to the Great Lakes Twin Ports, Duluth and Superior. Three players could sit in the front, three in the middle, and three in the back. Two jump seats behind the front seat were folded down and offered to the next game's starting pitcher so he could lie down and get some uncramped rest, according to Chester Morgan, who often drove one of the cars (player-manager Bill Adair drove the other). "They'd go about eighty miles per hour, and that's what we drove them. It was really scary. I figured if I was going to die I'd die behind the wheel."

One night, first baseman Dick Engquist was stopped by a state patrol-man in Minnesota for driving one of the Chryslers about eighty miles per hour. Engquist began to plead his case to the officer, saying he was just a poor baseball player. Unfortunately, Engquist didn't look like a Class C baseball player. "He had on green slacks, yellow and green alligator shoes, a big straw hat, and was smoking a big, black cigar. He looked like the biggest high roller you'd ever seen. The cop was unfazed," pitcher Ken Reitmeier recalled.

The Northern League had eight teams in 1952, and the one farthest from Eau Claire was 416 miles away in Grand Forks. On the way home from Fargo in July, one of the cars broke down in Littlefield, Minnesota, and four of the players were stranded, pitchers Ken Reitmeier and Bobby Brown, outfielder Lantz Blaney, and infielder Bob MacConnell. It took several days for the team to arrange to get the players back to Eau Claire.

Life on the road never was easy. In Sioux Falls the Bears had to dress in their hotel room before heading out to low-budget Howard Wood Field, home of the Canaries. The wooden grandstand extended down the foul lines well beyond the bases because the multipurpose facility was used for football and track, which included hosting the Dakota Relays. In fact, the running track went between the dugouts and foul lines, curved behind home plate and right field, and came back into the baseball field in left. A snow fence topped with about four feet of wire made up the outfield fence, which was so hard to see that umpires occasionally ruled home runs as ground rule doubles. Balls that carried over the fence would sometimes bounce on the running track, but umpires thought they had bounced first to get over the fence. "We got used to it," said Len Vandehey, an All-Star right fielder for Sioux Falls.

Once that season the Bears played a doubleheader at Chiefs Park in Grand Forks, hit the road for eight hours, and played a doubleheader the next night in Eau Claire. Aaron, who was known for his ability to sleep while on the road, was 6-for-16 in the four games. Aaron often would crawl into the corner back seat and sleep through most of the trips, Morgan recalled. Another time, the Bears drove all night after a game in Eau Claire and arrived in Fargo at 6 A.M. They went to their hotel expecting to get some sleep, but Adair informed them that the first of their two games that day was at 10 A.M., so the weary players got some breakfast and headed straight to the field.

The toughest trip of the season for Aaron, Bowers, and Wes Covington may have been to Aberdeen, where a hotel owner refused to house the three black players. The Bears then stayed at a hotel out of town. "I give Bill Adair credit for saying the whole team won't stay if the blacks can't," Reitmeier said. Several players remember that in other cities Aaron, Bowers, and Covington stayed in a separate hotel. If black players weren't treated well in Aberdeen, then that season must have been a very long one for Aberdeen third baseman Luis Garcia of Venezuela and shortstop

Roosevelt Evans. Both were black. As a hitter, however, Aaron had to love Aberdeen Municipal Ball Park, where it was just 291 feet down both foul lines. In one game early in the season, fifteen home runs were hit. But in the six games he played that season at Aberdeen, Aaron didn't hit any home runs. At age eighteen he didn't have a home run swing and wasn't concerned about swinging for the fences.

Traveling in any part of Northern League territory never was easy. In 1933 Eau Claire's first Bears hit the road in two seven-passenger Stude-bakers that previously had been owned by an undertaker. In the late 1950s Bears team cars suffered nine broken windshields while traveling through North Dakota, where pheasants were thick by the roadsides. The players would be driving along, some half asleep, when there would be a flutter of wings from the shadows in the ditch, a crash, feathers flying, and a large, colorful bird dead in someone's lap. Usually it hit the unlucky driver, a frugal ballplayer who got an extra ten dollars a month to drive the car and endure such attacks.

By the time Joe Torre played for the Braves in 1960, the Northern League teams included Winnipeg, Canada, and Minot, North Dakota. Being on the far eastern side of the league boundaries, Eau Claire teams had the longest trips: 416 miles to Grand Forks, 552 to Winnipeg, and a stomach-cramping twelve-to-fourteen-hour, 632-mile marathon to Minot. The Eau Claire Braves of 1960 traveled in red Chevrolet station wagons with the Milwaukee Braves logo proudly displayed on the door. One of the road-weary players once figured that if the team took a wrong turn leaving Eau Claire and traveled the 600-plus miles to the east they would end up four miles beyond Pittsburgh's Forbes Field.

In addition to being in another country, Winnipeg certainly offered the most contrasts in the league. It was the farthest point from civilization yet the biggest city in the league, with a population of two hundred thousand. It had one of the best stadiums, which seated thirty-five hundred people, and the coldest climate. But during the summer months its far northern location meant the sun didn't go down until very late in the evening. Games that began at 8 P.M. did not need lights. It wasn't the land of the midnight sun but pretty close. In 1933 a league record was set at Winnipeg's Sherbourne Stadium when Winnipeg defeated Eau Claire 35–19, for a total of fifty-four runs. A strong wind blew many balls about the park and over the fence, but despite forty-nine hits the game was completed in just two hours and forty minutes, or about the time that Major League managers today make their first of two to four late-inning pitching changes in a 3–2 game. A game like that today might take six hours. In the early years of the league, ballparks had no lights so games were played in the afternoon or twilight. Two times in Winnipeg visiting players died during twilight games when they were hit in the face by pitched balls. Those were the days before batting helmets. At the turn of the twenty-first century, baseball still was popular way up north. Winnipeg was back in the modern Northern League with a new stadium and, finally, lights.

The minor leagues gave players plenty of incentive to improve. After one experience of playing a doubleheader in Winnipeg, driving all night and half the next day back to Eau Claire, then heading to Carson Park by 5 P.M. for a night game, who wouldn't want to get out of there, no matter how nice it was? Who wouldn't want to either get to the majors as fast as possible or get on the next Greyhound headed for home, where Dad had a nine-to-five job waiting at the family store, where the best looking girl in town who fell in love with the best athlete in town was waiting impatiently, where you could live a comfortable if boring life on a tree-lined street, including batter-fried fish and fries and a few beers on Friday nights at the Wagon Wheel. Although it was billed as one of the best Class C minor leagues in the country, playing in the Northern League surely meant little more to players than getting to first base. Eau Claire wasn't a destination for minor leaguers; it was a proving ground.

Eventually some teams in the old Northern League upgraded from big cars to small buses that held fifteen to eighteen players. On the sunny Saturday morning of July 24, 1948, the team from Duluth set off in their bus from Eau Claire heading to Saint Cloud to continue a road trip. On Highway 36 in Saint Paul, a large truck crossed the center line on a rise in the road and hit the bus almost head-on. Both vehicles burst into flames. Five people died: three players, Duluth manager George Treadwell, and the truck driver. Seven players were critically injured. Of the fourteen players who survived, only four ever played baseball again. One of them was Albert "Red" Schoendienst, who played nineteen years in the majors—including 1957 to 1960 with Aaron and the Braves—and made the Hall of Fame in 1989.

After Eau Claire's Braves folded in 1962, the Northern League played nine more seasons, although teams gradually dropped out, leaving just four in the terminal year. For twenty-two years, as minor league ball underwent changes across the country, there was no minor league in the Upper Midwest, the onetime hotbed for prospects. Then entrepreneur Miles Wolff formed another Northern League in 1993—sixty years after the original—but made sure this one wouldn't be dragged down by the Major League clubs. This time the Northern League would be independent, the first of its kind in modern baseball. It would be free to rise or fall on its ability to find quality baseball players and to market the game to a public that was disenchanted with aspects of Major League Baseball in the 1990s—domes, contract disputes, union squabbles, player strikes, rising ticket prices, and petulant players. Baseball analyst Peter Gammons said the new Northern League is "the American dream without the bureaucracy of the baseball owners who have messed up the game."

The Northern League allows ex–major leaguers, ex-minor leaguers, and rookies. Teams are allowed four players with four years of pro experience. Every time one of the Northern League's players makes it to the majors, or in the case of the ex–major leaguers who make it back to the majors, trumpets blare from the teams' public relations departments to remind fans that they are seeing baseball at a level comparable to Class AA or even AAA. In the first five years, the Northern League sold 150 players to Major League organizations. The arrangement is much like the post–Jackie Robinson Negro League, which developed players and then sold them for a profit to Major League teams.

YANKEES AND SAINTS

On August 19, 1998, I headed for Saint Paul, ninety miles west of Eau Claire, to see the marquee team of the newest Northern League, the Saint Paul Saints, play the Thunder Bay Whiskey Jacks. But first I'd stop at the Hubert H. Humphrey Metrodome across the metroplex where the Minnesota Twins were playing the New York Yankees. I wanted to interview Aaron's old Braves teammate Joe Torre before the game and planned to leave in time to see the Saints game outdoors. After all, it was a summer evening.

The Yankees were having one of the best seasons in baseball history with Torre as their manager. He already was famous in New York for having led the team to the 1996 World Series crown. He was enjoying all the fruits of being a champion in New York because the team was winning in a way not seen since Babe Ruth, Lou Gehrig, Joe DiMaggio, Yogi Berra, Mickey Mantle, and Reggie Jackson. Torre had written a book. A movie was made about him. His face was popping up in national TV commercials and at parties with President Clinton. He previously had been forgettable as a coach despite a great Major League career. Torre had been fired three times as a manager and had been in more games than any other manager without reaching the World Series. All the setbacks seemed to spell finis to his career. At fifty-five, he was down to his last strike—working broadcasts of Little League World Series games. Then George Steinbrenner of the Yankees called and asked him to come home—home to New York. Torre had rooted against the Yankees when growing up, Steinbrenner was hell to work for, going through managers like disposable contacts, and the media in New York love to be merciless. Against his better judgment, he went.

At 4:15 P.M. I went looking for Torre in the visiting locker room, at first encountering a TV interview in session in the hallway with ex-Twin Chuck Knoblauch, who was saying how happy and lucky he was to be in New York, where the Yankees were in baseball Camelot with a 92-30 record, best in history after just 122 games. "This is a once-in-a-lifetime thing," Knoblauch said. Assistant coach Don Zimmer, looking as jowly as he does on TV, walked by with a bat in his hands. With his beer-barrel middle and short strides, he was a carnival mirror version of Babe Ruth. Yankees stars Paul O'Neill and Derek Jeter—combined annual salary $11.25 million—went into the locker room.

I—who assuredly will make less than 20 percent of that salary in a career of journalism—then followed. I felt a little out of place among the high-priced heroes and quickly asked where I could find Torre. An attendant told me he was in a small side room, and I walked in. Torre was watching the Cubs game on TV and hitching up his pants as he dressed for the game. I suspected this wasn't a good time to talk. He glanced at me, and obviously needing some privacy, quietly asked a team official, whose job must be precisely this—to protect Torre's privacy while dressing—what I wanted. He would be available for a group interview at 5 P.M. in the dugout, I was told, and maybe available for a few one-on-one questions after that.

I could handle free time now that I was in the locker room of one of baseball's greatest teams ever. I was eager to touch the Yankee greatness. My first hero had been Mickey Mantle. My first team (I was age six when the Braves left Wisconsin and twelve when the Brewers came) was the Yankees. I loved the deep blue. Now all around me was the color behind the stars in the United States flag. The Yankees stand for America, their success symbolic with American greatness. I was forty years old but still excited to be in a New York Yankees locker room for the first time in my life, even though I was nearly a generation older than some of these men. People age, but dreams don't.

I introduced myself to Paul O'Neill and asked him what made Torre such a good coach. "He can smile when times are tough. A lot of coaches don't do that," he replied. Another Yankee with Eau Claire connections came by—pitching coach Tony Cloninger, who was with the Eau Claire Braves in 1958. He recalled being in Eau Claire "long enough to start nine

Tony Cloninger played for the Eau Claire Braves in 1958 and later played with Henry Aaron for the Milwaukee Braves.

(Photo courtesy of the *Eau Claire Leader-Telegram*)

and lose nine. I went to the barber after I lost the eighth or ninth game. He said, 'You bonus babies don't have it in this league.' It was the shortest haircut I ever had." His Eau Claire experience must have seemed worse than it was; actually Cloninger was 2-2 in Eau Claire. He went on to have a decent Major League career (113-97 record), was with Cincinnati's Big Red Machine in the 1970s, and played with Aaron eight years in Milwaukee and Atlanta. His locker was next to Aaron's. "I played with Johnny Bench and Pete Rose. Henry was the best hitter I've seen in my lifetime. He helped me a lot as a pitcher, just listening to him talk about hitting. A lot of things people don't say was he stole thirty-five bases a year and was a good outfielder. I can't say enough about him," Cloninger said, as he leaned against the subterranean wall in the half-light, his Yankee uniform bulging at the midsection. Cloninger must have learned a few things about hitting from Aaron too. He hit two grand slams in a game in 1966, tying a Major League record, and had nine RBIs for the game, a Major League record for pitchers. The previous year he won twenty-four games for the Braves. He was getting good haircuts in those days.

At 4:45 P.M. reserve second baseman Homer Bush was in the locker room entryway talking not too seriously on the telephone with his fielding glove on his head. Next to him was a table full of energy food—an industrial-size jar of Jif peanut butter, two loaves of bread, Power Bars, bananas, Pop-Tarts and a toaster, jelly, and coffee. Yankees beat reporters hovered around star players as other players dressed or signed their names to shirts and balls for charitable causes, or so they were told. Three large blue canvas bags stood against the wall near the entryway, each stuffed with about thirty bats. Nearby were two blue trunks filled with more bats. O'Neill came over, hoisted a few, and left for the field, the locker room door closing on the rattling wood. In the far end of the room a half-dozen Yankees leaned back on folding chairs and watched the Cubs play Saint Louis on a wall-mounted TV. Darryl Strawberry sat in the dark corner smoking a cigarette and talking to a man in a pin-striped suit. Two months later, Strawberry would be recovering from surgery to remove a two-and-a-half-inch cancerous tumor from his intestine. In the summer of 2000, he needed more treatment after the disease returned. Between bouts of cancer, he and the Yankees won a World Series and he was suspended from baseball for the third time for violating its drug policy—the result of testing positive for cocaine use.

Midway down one wall in the room was more to eat and drink, a bar with Budweiser, Bud Light, beef jerky, potato chips, granola bars, and a plethora of candy bars and jars filled with Tootsie Rolls and Hot Tamales and Jolly Ranchers. My childhood neighborhood grocery store didn't stock as much candy. Near the beer taps was a double-wide upright cooler with sliding glass doors that chilled soda, milk, fruit juice, energy drinks, and mineral water—cases of it. Baseball players who learn to be selective as hitters must apply that ability to their eating habits. Most people offered all this free food and drink day after day wouldn't have 7 percent body fat and be able to go from home to third base without suffering oxygen deprivation. Or even be able to go from first to third. Babe Ruth used to eat seven hot dogs and drink a beer before a game; where in the world would he draw the line if all this free food faced him day after day?

After the game, it's more food. The Major League custom now is to offer players a fully catered postgame meal courtesy of the home team. Torre remembers that in 1957, when he went into the Braves locker room in Milwaukee with his brother Frank after a World Series game, the only food available was cheese and crackers, the only drinks were beer and Coca-Cola, and the players had to record what they took so they could reimburse the team. These days nobody wants to offend the baseball players, some of the richest men in the nation, so their cornucopia always is overflowing Thanksgiving-style. What team would want to be criticized by the New York Yankees as having questionable locker room service? Nobody wants to be seen as cheap these days; it's bad for public relations.

The media had descended on Orlando "El Duque" Hernandez, the Cuban pitching star with the don't-try-this-at-home (especially those over forty) high leg kick. He was using relief pitcher and Panama native Mariano Rivera as an interpreter. The serious conversation lasted fifteen minutes, interrupted only when one player leaned over and efficiently cleared a nostril into a nearby trash can as one finger was pressed against the opposite nostril. Another player then used the can as a spittoon. Mark McGwire hit home runs number forty-eight and forty-nine, the Cards won 8–6 in ten innings, the TV went off, and the Yankees went out to play inside.

At 5:05 P.M. I walked onto the spongy Metrodome artificial turf. Early-arriving fans crowded into the front row of the stands near the Yankees dugout and held out pens and balls and hats to be signed. The Yankees didn't oblige. I looked at the ultrarich ballplayers and wondered if they ever thought how far removed their lives are from the fans' lives, wondered if would they spend two dollars on a Coke or three dollars on a hot dog if they made only twenty-five thousand dollars a year. Sunflower seed shells littered the turf. Yankees were all about the no-trespassing zone, taking batting practice, a flamingolike flock of them stretching in unison with huge rubber bands, a baseball ballet set to seventies Doobie Brothers, "Rocking Down the Highway," on the stadium PA system. Some sat on the bench. They do this 162 times a year, not counting spring training, in search of sports' Holy Grail, the World Series ring, in search of perfect throws and perfect swings and, nowadays, perfect paychecks. Twenty-four hours earlier, they did it in Kansas City. These Yankees were approaching perfection. They were being compared with the best team of all time, the 1927 Yankees, who won 110 games and the World Series behind Ruth's record-setting sixty home runs. By the end of the season, the 1998 Yankees had won 114 of 162 games, setting an American League record and second only in baseball history to 116 games won by the 1906 Cubs. They won the World Series in four games, for which they each received a bonus check of $320,000, the diamond ring—and more free food in the playoffs.

At 5:10 P.M. Torre arrived and twelve reporters converged on him in the dugout. He's dressed for the game and nonchalantly answers low-key questions that get even lower key as the session drags on. He's asked about the rough airplane landing in a storm in Minneapolis the night before. "We flew sideways there for a while. I was waiting for Leslie Nielsen to walk out. It's as hard a landing as I've ever been involved in." A reporter asks an obviously stupid question hoping for a sound bite from Torre. "If the pilot was a player, would you send him back to Columbus?" The subject turns somehow to school, and Torre says he hated it. Then the subject turns inexplicably to golf, and he says he has a tee time Saturday morning in Texas. The reporters are riveted on Torre as he sits against the back of the dugout and watches warmups. A stray ball bounces into his lap. Torre seems oddly comfortable talking about mundane topics when the reporters obviously are hoping to pick up some nugget of information that might help them break a story on the hottest team in baseball. No such luck tonight.

At 5:40 P.M. they wander off and Torre talks to me about Eau Claire and 1960. First to mind isn't baseball but the two-story house with an apartment where he and two teammates, Paul Roof and Paul Chenger, stayed for five dollars a week, including laundry service. The house, at 627 Menomonie Street on the north bank of the Chippewa River, was run by a big, boisterous strawberry blonde Irish woman, Georgiana "Ma" Farwell. A legend among players in Eau Claire, she was not only their house mother but came to all the games, rang a cowbell, and hooted and hollered for her young Braves. Often she chided them that they were chasing after the local girls as much as fly balls. One time, the players helped Ma stage a practical joke. Using her bellowing voice, she often hurled verbal insults at local umpiring legend Ham Olive (who was behind the plate for Aaron's first game in Eau Claire). The players arranged to get Ma down on the field for a sneak attack. With an umbrella in hand, she chased Olive around the field to the delight of the players and fans.

Farwell always was up to greet her Braves in the middle of the night when they arrived home from a road trip, with her famous eggshell-in-the-grounds coffee on the stove and a pile of fresh cinnamon rolls on the table. During the day, it wasn't uncommon to find up to twenty children or Ma's friends hanging out around the house, waiting to see the players or just to see what was happening. If they went out back, they probably could find Torre sixty feet six inches away from Chenger, a pitcher, playing catch. Ma gave the okay and let her husband, who was in landscaping, haul in enough black dirt for a backyard pitcher's mound. Torre must have remembered the kindnesses. For more than twenty years after he left Eau Claire, he called Ma Farwell on December 24 to wish her a merry Christmas.

Torre, who signed with the Milwaukee Braves for forty thousand dollars, had a great season in Eau Claire playing catcher. He led the league in hitting, with a .344 average, and possibly in weight, at 225 pounds. He drove in seventy-four runs and hit sixteen homers, and he was a Northern League All-Star and Rookie of the Year, just like Aaron. Torre beat out future major leaguer Max Alvis of Minot by one percentage point for the batting crown when he got six hits in a doubleheader on the final day of the season. "Eau Claire was a complete joy for me," he said. Except when his temper got the best of him and he got thrown out of six games by a young umpire named Bruce Froemming. "We were both spoiled kids," Torre said. Froemming, a Milwaukee native, umpired in the Northern League in 1959 and 1960 then went on to become a crew chief in the National League.

Torre met another Italian American in Eau Claire, Sam Cifaldi, the son of Italian immigrants and owner of Sammy's Pizza, the first and only pizzeria in town, on North Barstow Street downtown. Torre and his friends went to Sammy's after games because Sam often gave them free thin-crust pizza, his specialty. They became such good friends that Sam let Joe use his car on dates, a gold 1957 two-door hardtop Chrysler New Yorker.

The team managers and umpires who came into Sammy's all said the same thing about Torre: He's headed to the big leagues. In 1998, thirty-eight years after they met, Sam Cifaldi went to a Yankees game at the Metrodome in Minneapolis to see Torre. He watched Torre run on the field with the team but didn't think he had a chance to get his attention in the cacophony of front-row autograph seekers. Then Sam's son Frank told him to shout "Sammy's Pizza!" and when he did that Joe turned and spotted him in the crowd. Torre ran—literally ran—over to greet Sam and renew acquaintances. "He's still the gentleman he was," said Sam, who works part time at his sons' Sammy's Pizza in Cumberland, Wisconsin. Sammy's Pizza in Eau Claire still exists (under new ownership), and the pizzas still are made in the front window just as in 1960. All that's missing are pro ballplayers looking for a postgame meal.

Catcher Joe Torre of Brooklyn, New York, was the Northern League Rookie of the Year for the Eau Claire Braves in 1960. At the end of the season, he was called up by the Milwaukee Braves and recorded his first Major League hit.

(Photo courtesy of the *Eau Claire Leader-Telegram*)

Torre's season got even better after he left Eau Claire in September of 1960 (he went to Sammy's to get boxes for packing). Torre drove to Milwaukee to meet with his brother Frank, who had been his hero as a kid, and planned to drive back to Brooklyn. He was summoned to the Braves offices and was shocked to find out they wanted him in uniform. On September 25, with his legs shaking, Joe pinch-hit for pitcher Warren Spahn at County Stadium and got a single in his first Major League at bat. In twelve months Torre had gone from the sandlots of Brooklyn to the Major Leagues. The next spring he spent twenty-seven games in the minors in Louisville before the Braves called him up for good. Torre made the majors at age twenty-one after one year in the minors. Aaron had made it at age twenty after two years.

In seventeen years in the majors Torre had a .297 average, more than twenty-three hundred hits and was the National League's MVP in 1971. He played with Aaron and the Braves through the 1968 season before being traded to Saint Louis. Unlike his brother, who got sent back to the minors from Milwaukee in 1960, Torre never had to go back to Eau Claire. He may be on his way to Cooperstown.

At 6:30 P.M. I was off to Saint Paul to see the Saints. Three of the new Northern League teams were in the league when Aaron played—Duluth-Superior, Fargo-Moorhead, and Sioux Falls. The Saints weren't in the old Northern League. They were part of the American Association from 1902 to 1960 and sent such players as Duke Snider and Roy Campanella to their parent club, the Brooklyn Dodgers.

I was eager to see Northern League baseball in the 1990s but not sure what to expect—baseball or comedy. One of the owners of the Saints is actor Bill Murray of *Saturday Night Live* and *Caddyshack* fame. Murray wore a Saints cap in the movie *Space Jam.* He has coached first and third base for the Saints many times, the Saints program proudly related. The president of the Saints is Mike Veeck. He is known—and proud to be—for arranging Disco Demolition Night in 1979 in Chicago, which turned into a riot and forced the White Sox to forfeit the game. His father, Bill, was an owner with three Major League teams, including the Saint Louis Browns, where he sent baseball purists into a frenzy when he inserted three-feet-seven, sixty-five-pound Eddie Gaedel into the lineup in 1951 as a publicity stunt. Gaedel walked and was pulled out for a pinch-runner, Jim Delsing, who played minor league ball in Eau Claire in 1946 but, alas, became famous only for this. Baseball has been such a conservative game throughout the century that this one stunt, which took all of a few minutes, still is talked about half a century later, still is infamous. In fact, as I perused the press notes prior to the Saints game, I saw that "Today in Baseball History," August 19, 1951, Eddie Gaedel made his famous ninety-foot walk into the history books. Appropriately, I was about to watch the next generation of Veeck family stunts on the anniversary of Eddie Gaedel's walk.

Despite the stunts, it's hard not to take the Saints seriously. They were managed by Marty Scott, who was director of the minor leagues for the Texas Rangers when they produced Major League stars such as Sammy Sosa, Ruben Sierra, and others. Obviously, Scott knew baseball. Darryl Strawberry, the New York Yankees star I had just seen in Minneapolis, was on his last legs as a major leaguer until he was signed by the Saints in 1996. He batted .435 and hit eighteen home runs in twenty-nine games with the Saints before the Yankees took notice. They signed him on July 4, and three days later he was in Yankees pinstripes and helping them reach and win the World Series. The next year the Saints landed J. D. Drew, the number one player in the college draft. He also hit eighteen home runs for the Saints before he ended a holdout and signed with the Saint Louis Cardinals in 1998. Drew, like Strawberry, went directly from the Northern League to the majors.

The new Northern League is considered Class A, but the Saints are in a league of their own. They sell out 6,329-seat Midway Stadium, which opened in 1957, night after night. By the end of this season they would draw their maximum of 270,000 fans, 90,000 ahead of second-place Fargo-Moorhead. Eau Claire's best season ever was 101,000 fans in 1949. The Saints have a waiting list for season tickets. What the stadium lacks in aesthetics—it's in a warehouse district sandwiched between multiple sets of busy railroad tracks—it makes up for in fun. That's why most Saints fans were there, it seemed, for the Bill Veeck–type gags. These have included a pig mascot that delivered balls to the umpire, sumo wrestling and spin-the-bat contests between innings, a sweatiest fan contest, a Gedney pickle race, and an irreverent PA announcer sitting in the window of the press box with his legs hanging out, deadpanning play-by-play like Bill Murray and playing word and sound games with players' names. Fans can get a haircut, a manicure, a massage, or a shower at the game. The action on the field seems secondary to whatever prank or one-liner is next. Midway Stadium seems an extension of the State Fair; a fair auditorium is a quarter-mile beyond the left-field fence. In the past the Saints have experimented with replays by live mimes between innings, a blind radio announcer, and—even more of an affront to decency than Eddie Gaedel—a tryout for a catcher with no legs. He didn't make the team.

The fans on this night were having fun. They included two men double-dating blonde twins—I suddenly craved Doublemint gum—and an obese man in a tank top and wide-brimmed hat balancing two overflowing plates of nachos, meat, and cheese on his beer cups as he slowly climbed the steps back to his seat. Is baseball as a spectator sport all about having fun or is it appreciating good baseball? The Saints were putting the question to the test. They had won two Northern League titles since 1993 and had fun doing it. The Midway was the center of a Saints baseball circus. One writer called it baseball's amusement park.

By the fourth inning, eight trains had rumbled past the left field wall, adding to the odd ambiance. By the fifth inning, I was headed back to Eau Claire, knowing that the baseball game might be good but that the gags were getting old. I never knew if I should watch the game or the sideshows or seek divine intervention—a massage from Sister Rosalind Gefre. I feared I might miss something cool if I concentrated on the ball-strike count. I get the same feeling when I'm at a shopping mall, my focus constantly diverted by flashing lights, weird music, and unusual people. I always get stressed out from the stimuli after about an hour and want to go home.

NORTH TO DULUTH

Two days later, my thirteen-year-old son, Jerad, and I were off on a weekend through the new Northern League. We would see the Duluth-Superior Dukes on Friday night and the Fargo-Moorhead Redhawks on Saturday night, with a stop on the way to visit an Eau Claire and Major League legend in northern Minnesota. Jerad had played Little League for three years but didn't follow Major League Baseball closely. I was curious about whether he would enjoy the games and whether other Northern League games were anything like Saint Paul's. With side trips, we would drive nearly nine hundred miles in three days. But it wouldn't be anything like the road trips of Henry Aaron's day. We had two people in a seven-person, air-conditioned minivan, and we didn't have to play ball once we arrived in each city. All we had to do was watch and listen.

We drove north through Indianhead Country, as northwestern Wisconsin is called because that quadrant of the state resembles the profile of an Indian chief when isolated on a map (probably so called by a lost tourist who stared at the map too long and lost focus). We were passing baseball history to our right and left. To our right, or east, was Three Lakes, the hometown of Cy Williams, the first player to hit two hundred home runs in American League history. To our left, or west, were the hometowns of Cubs-Dodgers-Braves star Andy Pafko (Boyceville) and the lesser known Ed Barney. In 1915 and 1916, Barney made the majors for eighty-eight games with the New York Yankees and the Pittsburgh Pirates, getting sixty-one hits and no home runs. He was born in Amery, Wisconsin, in 1890 and died in Rice Lake in 1967.

Farther west was Saint Croix Falls, the home of Roy Patterson, a spitball pitcher who has a niche in Major League history like that of another Polk County native and spitballer, Burleigh Grimes. On April 24, 1901, the rookie Patterson (who was born in Stoddard, Wisconsin) was the winning pitcher as the Chicago White Stockings defeated Cleveland 8–2 in Chicago in the first game in American League history. Patterson pitched a complete game and gave up six hits. The game is considered the first in A.L. history because the other three games scheduled that day were rained out. On the fiftieth anniversary celebration of the American League, baseball legends Clark Griffith and Connie Mack asked Patterson who won the first-ever league game. Patterson didn't know it was he. Often called the Saint Croix Falls Boy Wonder, Patterson won twenty games in 1901 and nineteen in 1902 before an injury ended his career in 1907. He retired in Saint Croix Falls and wound up coaching two teams in the Northern League, including Winnipeg. When Patterson died in 1953, New York *Herald Tribune* sports writer Red Smith wrote, "If a rookie pitcher came up to the American League today and won 20 games in his first season and 20 games in his second you'd sort of expect him to be remembered. Christy Mathewson didn't break in like that, nor did Walter Johnson, nor Rube Waddell, nor Ed Walsh, nor Carl Hubbell, and they're all remembered."

Looking to our right again was Birchwood, Wisconsin, the retirement home of Fred Thomas and the home of a coveted piece of national baseball memorabilia. In 1918 Thomas played third base on the last Boston Red Sox team of the twentieth century to win the World Series. It was an odd season for Thomas, a twenty-five-year-old rookie from Milwaukee who played forty-four games, then went into the service all summer at the Great Lakes Naval Training Station near Chicago. It also was an odd year for baseball, which played a shortened schedule because of World War I. The Red Sox took the American League pennant with seventy-five wins, despite problems at third base. Red Sox manager Ed Barrow kept Thomas on the roster and was able to get a furlough for him so he could start in the Series against the Chicago Cubs. "I don't know what good I can do you," Thomas told Barrow. "I haven't seen big league pitching in three months." Thomas handled sixteen balls without an error and had two hits in the six-game Series, one more hit than a young, talented teammate, George Herman "Babe" Ruth. Ruth won two games on the mound and played left field, going 1-for-5 at the plate, the one hit being a two-run triple. It was the last World Series without a home run. Before the sixth game, the Red Sox posed for a team photo in Fenway Park, the slim Ruth

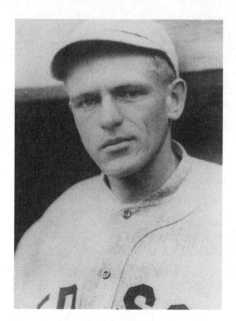

Wisconsin native Fred Thomas played third base in 1918 for the Boston Red Sox when they won their last World Series of the twentieth century. One of Thomas's teammates was Babe Ruth.

(Photo courtesy of the *Eau Claire Leader-Telegram*)

standing with his arms crossed directly behind the kneeling Thomas, a 140-pound man nicknamed "Rabbit" for his speed. In 1919 Thomas was traded to Philadelphia, one of the casualties of the Red Sox owners' deal that split up the team and sent Babe Ruth to the Yankees. Some people still believe that the trade spawned the "Curse of the Bambino," which has kept the Red Sox, who won five of the first fifteen World Series, from winning another one in the past eighty-plus seasons.

Troubled with what he thought was diabetes (but turned out not to be), Thomas retired in 1925 to Birchwood on Big Chetac Lake. At an uncle's urging he bought some land, and with his wife, Constance, opened Peep O' Dawn resort. Today called Fred Thomas Resort, it is still run by the family. His sons, Warren and Robert, live just down the lakeshore. Warren says that Fred played town ball for many years around Birchwood before he died in 1986. He often told stories about going out on the town with the free-spending Babe Ruth ("He'd spend money all right, but he'd spend your money"), trying to hit against Walter Johnson, being traded for Tris Speaker, playing for manager Connie Mack, and getting cussed out by Ty Cobb.

He also left behind a small, round legacy—a ball signed by Ruth and most other members of the 1918 Red Sox. Warren Thomas keeps it in a bank in nearby Rice Lake. It may be the only such ball from the 1918 team in existence, still valuable even though the Thomas children played with it for years and even though their mother, finally realizing its value, touched up some of the signatures. "Cooperstown wants it. The Boston sports museum wants it," Warren Thomas said. "I get calls all the time from collectors."

A few miles to the west, Clear Lake, the home of Burleigh Grimes, held too much baseball knowledge to just drive by. Grimes died in 1985 and is buried under a big spruce tree in the little northwestern Wisconsin town where he played his first baseball game and gave his last autograph. Yet Grimes won't be forgotten, not as long as his best friend, Chuck Clark, is still alive, and not as long as there's a museum in Clear Lake. In the city's old schoolhouse are theme rooms about the two most famous native sons, Grimes and Gaylord Nelson, former governor of Wisconsin, United States senator, and founder of Earth Day.

If you have a few hours, Clark, a retired lifelong city resident, will tell you story after story about "Old Stubblebeard" and "The Last of the

Spitball Pitchers," who made baseball history and witnessed it, who never forgot his small-town roots, who was the best friend Clark ever had. "I wouldn't take a million dollars for what I got. It's been the fun of a lifetime for me." The bond between Grimes and Clark is easy to see in Clark's house and in the Clear Lake Area Historical Museum. In both places, hundreds of Grimes's mementos line the walls, occupy the corners, and fill the display cases, shelves, and drawers to overflowing. Clark's photo-filled den is a collage of Hall of Famers. He likes to say that whenever a Hall of Famer dies, he looks up on his wall for the picture of the departed, and there he is smiling down on him.

No one is more proud to say he was Burleigh Grimes's friend than Clark. It was a friendship that began about 1960 and grew stronger when Grimes returned to nearby Lake Holcombe and then Clear Lake to live the final years of his life. The two became inseparable. Grimes gained a personal secretary and historian. Clark, whose father had died when he was thirteen, gained a father figure who happened to know everything about and everybody in baseball. They were together in 1964 when Grimes was inducted into the Hall of Fame in Cooperstown. Clark will never forget Grimes crying hours after the induction and saying, "That plaque—that's for all of us up there." Clark knew that Grimes was referring to all the people of tiny Clear Lake, population 950.

For many years, Clark and his wife, Ardith, accompanied Grimes and his wife to Hall of Fame ceremonies as well as autograph sessions around the country. Those events let Clark hear baseball tales firsthand, get rare autographs, and become friends with retired stars like Ted Williams and Bob Feller. Clark still corresponds regularly with Feller, the Iowa farm boy whose hundred-mile-per-hour fastball made him famous with the Cleveland Indians in the 1940s. When Feller had a limited edition bronze cast made of his famous fastball grip—complete with autographed ball— he sent one to Clark in 1997.

Clark has hundreds of autographed balls, photos, and mementos from Hall of Famers such as Williams, Satchel Paige, Roger Maris, Mickey Mantle, and many others. His thousand-volume baseball library has numerous books about Ted Williams, all signed by Williams. In a corner of Clark's den is a lamp made from part of a bronzed baseball bat and glove. Grimes once used those pieces of equipment in a World Series.

And one of Clark's greatest thrills came each year at Hall of Fame ceremonies when he was routinely mistaken for his lookalike, former Minnesota Twins slugger Harmon Killebrew. He gave up trying to tell people he wasn't Killebrew and just waved back.

None of the autographs or other thrills meant as much to Clark, however, as being Grimes's friend. Clark and Grimes were of the same cloth. They were Clear Lake natives, neighbors on a quiet street, and lovers of America's pastime. In summer Clark used to sit on Grimes's back porch as Grimes smoked his pipe, drank ice water, and talked about World Series games and famous plays long ago. Friends and town residents out for a walk would stop by and Grimes would invite them in for a signature and a visit. Grimes would recall that beyond his back porch was the school field where he played his first baseball game and that when he played for the Clear Lake team as a teenager, his father, the coach, wouldn't let him pitch in home games because he didn't think Burleigh was good enough.

They would recall that Grimes's Major League career began in 1916 with the Pittsburgh Pirates, as a teammate of Hall of Fame shortstop Honus Wagner, and ended in 1934 with the New York Yankees, which had Ruth and Lou Gehrig, with nineteen seasons of spitballs in between.

Grimes was considered one of baseball's fiercest competitors. "Show me a guy who can lose easy and he ain't going to be a winner," Grimes once told Clark. In fact, baseball's most feared competitor, Ty Cobb, once was asked to make up a team of players he'd like to have in a big game. He chose Grimes as his pitcher. "A gruff, hard-bitten type, he was only too willing to knock down any batter with the temerity to dig in at the plate," the editors of *Total Baseball* said of him.

Grimes was the classic farm boy who made it big in the big city, a lot of big cities—Pittsburgh, Brooklyn, New York, Saint Louis, Chicago. To Brooklyn fans, he was simply "Boily." He compiled a 270-212 record, making him one of the winningest pitchers of all time. He won twenty games or more in five seasons (leading the league with twenty-five wins in 1928) and had thirty-five shutouts.

No question Grimes was great. For example, in the 1920s when there were future Hall of Fame pitchers such as Dazzy Vance, Lefty Grove, and Walter Johnson, Grimes led the majors in victories, complete games, and innings pitched. He was number two in strikeouts.

Personal statistics were only part of the story. Grimes played in four World Series. In 1920 he led the Brooklyn Dodgers to a runner-up finish in the World Series with a 23-11 record. When that season ended, Grimes and the Dodgers—which also included future Hall of Famers Zack Wheat and Rube Marquard—went on a barnstorming tour of the country. On October 13, 1920, he brought the Dodgers to Rice Lake, Wisconsin, not far from Clear Lake, for an exhibition game, according to a handbill in the Clear Lake museum. The Dodgers also played a game that week in Chippewa Falls, losing 5–4 to a team from Augusta, Wisconsin.

In 1931 Grimes led Saint Louis to a championship with a 17-9 record. In the World Series he had a two-hit shutout in game three, outdueling Lefty Grove. In game seven he went eight and two-thirds innings and held off Philadelphia 4–2 for the title. Grimes's Series-clinching win was only half the story. He won despite pitching with an inflamed appendix, which was iced down between innings. He shut out the Athletics for eight innings and gave up two runs in the ninth before a relief pitcher recorded the final out. That game may have been the highlight of Grimes's career. At age thirty-eight he was hailed as a hero in headlines across the nation. His teammates carried him from the field. In his will Grimes bequeathed his beloved 1931 World Series ring to someone who would truly appreciate it—Chuck Clark.

Grimes retired after the 1934 season, part of which he played with Babe Ruth, Lou Gehrig, and the Yankees. A ball signed by all three is in the Clear Lake museum. Grimes's final spitter was thrown in one inning of relief pitching. Grimes's retirement at age forty-one officially ended baseball's spitball era. The spitball—a pitch that supposedly danced when moistened with saliva—was outlawed in 1920, but seventeen players could continue to use that pitch because they already were in the league. Grimes was the last of those men to retire.

But 1934 wasn't the end of his career. Grimes took up coaching and scouting. He coached the Brooklyn Dodgers in 1937 and 1938. Among his assistants were Ruth and Leo Durocher. A picture of the threesome hangs on Clark's den wall. The Dodgers uniform was the last that Ruth wore. Ruth often came up in Clark's conversations with Grimes. When asked to pick out the greatest players of his era, Grimes would say, "God gave it all to that guy. The rest of us had to work for it."

Ruth is the only player that Grimes ever came close to criticizing, Clark said. Grimes always spoke highly of the men he played against. Once, however, he began to say something negative about Ruth's personal life, then stopped, looked at Clark, and said, "But don't ever question his ability."

Grimes's only head coaching job was with the Dodgers, although he also coached several minor league teams in the 1930s, '40s, and '50s. Grimes also scouted for the Yankees, Kansas City Athletics, and Baltimore Orioles until leaving baseball for good about 1970.

Then he returned to Wisconsin. During his final years, whenever Grimes was paid to attend autograph sessions, he told the promoter to make a check out to the Clear Lake museum. The local high school team now plays its games at Grimes Field.

When Grimes threw his last spitball in 1934, it was the end of an era in more ways than one. Babe Ruth hit his 700th home run that summer and was in the final months of his career. Two Ruthian babies were born in 1934, Henry Aaron and Roger Maris.

In 1984, fifty years after he threw the last legal spitball in the Major Leagues, Burleigh Grimes revealed the secret of his famous pitch to *Life* magazine. Grimes said the key to the spitter was mixing slippery elm bark with his saliva. "I'd put a piece of bark in my mouth to make the saliva thicker. Then I'd release the ball like I was squeezing a watermelon pit. Hell, I can teach anybody to throw one in ten minutes. What's hard is controlling the damn thing. Why, some games the spitter was my best pitch, and other days it would break my heart." It broke his heart in the fifth game of the 1920 World Series. In the first inning, Elmer Smith of Cleveland hit a Grimes spitball for the first grand slam in Series history. In the fourth inning, Grimes let Jim Bagby become the first pitcher in Series history to hit a home run.

Grimes never forgot his roots when it came to his spitter. He threw his first pro spitters for Eau Claire in the minor leagues in 1912, and his last ones were moistened with the bark of slippery elm from trees that grew near Neillsville, Wisconsin, about fifty miles southeast of Eau Claire. At the end of his career, Neillsville was the only place he could find just the right bark to give his pitches some bite.

Grimes died of cancer in 1985 at the age of ninety-two but not before shakily signing one last autograph in bed in a book called *Baseball's Greatest Pitchers*. Fittingly, the book featured a chapter on Grimes. The autograph was for Clark. Although he has hundreds of items signed by some of baseball's greatest players, that signature is Clark's favorite. It may have been the final chapter of Grimes's life, but as long as Chuck Clark is around, the book on Burleigh Grimes never will be closed.

We made our first stop of the Northern League weekend along Highway 35 in Webster, Wisconsin, pulling into the local drive-in restaurant for a hamburger and french fries. There was no escaping baseball. Webster is the hometown of Jarrod Washburn, a six-feet-one, 196-pound pitcher for the Anaheim Angels. He too had made the big time and by 2001 was considered one of the top southpaws in the American League.

The small time was just up the road. Much like Midway Stadium in Saint Paul, we found Wade Stadium in the oldest part of Duluth, not far from the railroad tracks and the aging waterfront buildings of Lake Superior. Nearby, hopper cars filled with taconite or iron ore were rumbling toward a ship and a distant port. The stadium opened in 1941, four years after Carson Park in Eau Claire. It too was a WPA project. It too had been remodeled for more than half a million dollars. This was the stadium from the old and the new Duluth-Superior Dukes, the same place where Aaron took the field. Back in those days, however, Duluth and Superior had their own teams. Wade Stadium, with high brick walls extending down the foul lines and a longer and higher grandstand (capacity forty-one hundred), felt at once bigger and cozier than Carson Park, although its industrial setting couldn't compare aesthetically. More important, it was much more alive. Excitement was in the air as fans anticipated a good ball game between their Dukes and the Explorers of Sioux City, Iowa.

Why were 3,221 fans backed up at the turnstiles to go to a Dukes game? The Dukes were defending Northern League champions. In 1997 they defeated the Winnipeg Goldeyes, another old Northern League team, in the fifth and deciding game of the championship series before a standing room only crowd of 4,269 at Wade Stadium. It was just like old times. Duluth won its first Northern League pennant in 1937. Joe DiMaggio even visited the city regularly in the 1940s—but only because his first wife, Dorothy Arnold, grew up there. The last time the old Dukes won a Northern League title was 1956, the year Bob Uecker played in Eau Claire. Attendance hadn't always been good in Duluth in 1998, but baseball was back. Box seats were only seven dollars, it was a perfect summer evening in the Twin Ports, it was Bernick's Pepsi Backpack Night for kids, and Ila Borders was pitching. It was Ila they came to see.

More than anything, Ila Borders, a woman pitcher in a men's game, was why the Dukes had their second three-thousand-plus crowd of the season (she had pitched for their first big crowd too). Borders had pitched for the Saints in 1997 without success and was sent to Duluth for utility infielder Keith English, who muttered, "I got traded for a girl." In Duluth, Borders was showing she could get batters out. In fact, she made history and won her first game on July 24 against Sioux Falls, 3–1, and at one point pitched twelve straight scoreless innings. Yet her earned run average was a poor 7.58 and people still wondered if she was there because she should be or because she was a put-fans-in-the-seats novelty—the first woman to pitch in, start, and win a men's professional baseball game. She was the first to do those same things in a men's college game as well. Twenty-three-year-old Borders was the reason that celebrity news reporter Mike Wallace and a crew from CBS's *60 Minutes* were at the game.

Jerad and I had seats about seven rows up on the third-base side just above the Explorers dugout, a good view for a killing, as it turned out. It soon became apparent that it wasn't Borders's night. She had recorded only four outs when she was pulled from the game in the second inning and in that time gave up seven runs, including three home runs. Two of the home runs were by Marty Neff, a muscular blond with a goatee and a swagger in his walk. His second home run easily cleared the 380-foot sign in centerfield and the 30-foot-high fence behind the sign, a shot of Great Lakes proportions. Borders's fast ball wasn't very fast, about seventy-eight miles per hour, and Neff was waiting for it. Chest out, Neff trotted back to the dugout wearing a look of male superiority. Twenty-six years after Billie Jean King beat Bobby Riggs in the Battle of the Sexes, new ground still was waiting to be broken.

The Explorers won 9–3, but afterward Borders was the center of attention. Several male Dukes players were picked to sign postgame autographs, but the fans began chanting Borders's name until she ran out of sight in the dugout, embarrassed by the attention. I was able to corner her for a few questions. Although she was five-feet-ten, 150 pounds—a larger-than-average woman—she looked small in her baseball uniform with her narrow face and shoulders. Her long hair, pulled back into a broad, curly ponytail, covered the name on the back of her uniform. She said she didn't pitch well, that all the attention since her first victory a month ago was taking its toll. She knew people saw her as a groundbreaker but, she

said, "I don't see it as a male-female issue. I never have." Maybe it wasn't
to her, but she had to notice that when she threw the first pitch of the
game for a strike the Explorers batter turned to his teammates and smiled
sheepishly, seemingly saying, "Geez, a woman just threw one past me."

Before the game, Borders brusquely said no to Wallace when he wanted
an interview. Now *60 Minutes* and Wallace were waiting, and Dukes
majority owner, president, and CEO Jim Wadley let me know about it. A
retired lieutenant commander in the United States Navy, Wadley knows
how to give orders. "I've got eight people out there from *60 Minutes* waiting," he said, implying that my time almost was up and that I wasn't as
important as *60 Minutes*. Off went Borders for another interview. Jerad
and I went into the Dukes locker room. Wadley soon was there too, and
he was smiling about the big crowd and all the media attention—good for
business—apparently not upset at all about the loss. The Dukes were running sixth out of eight teams in league attendance, and they would draw
only seventy thousand for the season, but this was a night to remember.

Dukes manager George Mitterwald, a former catcher with the Minnesota Twins and Chicago Cubs, drank a beer in the locker room and
explained that Borders's pitches were up in the strike zone and that no
pitcher could get away with that no matter how fast they pitch. He stuck
up for Borders, saying slow pitchers can succeed in pro ball. When asked
if Borders belonged in the league, he said, "I'm not going to get into that."
But Sioux City coach Ed Nottle did. "Every time she pitches it hurts
the integrity of the league." I wondered how Mike Cuellar, the 1969 Cy
Young winner for the Baltimore Orioles who won almost two hundred
games in his career, felt about Borders. He was Borders's pitching coach
for the Dukes, but I couldn't find him.

Pro baseball in the 1990s was much more complex than baseball in the
1950s, a lot like pretty much everything in America. Ministers, pilots,
judges, police officers, congressmen, soldiers, firefighters, lawyers, secretar-
ies, nurses, stay-at-home parents, and on and on weren't all men or women
anymore. But Major League Baseball still was an all-male fraternity.

The Dukes locker room was a men's club. Dukes players sat around
loosely clothed after the game, eating sandwiches and watching TV, but
Borders showered and changed alone in her own locker area. The men
weren't worried she might visit. On the men's side was "Iron Man" Mike
Meggers, a ruggedly built young man who once played AAA ball in the

Cincinnati Reds system and was hoping the Northern League would be his new ticket to the Major Leagues. Every time Meggers came to bat that night, the throaty rock lyrics "I am IRONNN MANNN!" reverberated as Meggers strode to and dug in at the plate. It was a great macho moment, and Meggers had to feel like Superman playing baseball with Superwoman. "Ila is a great person and tough competitor," said Meggers, eating a cold meat sandwich, sitting on an old, dirty couch and wearing only a towel over his midsection. "She really wants to do well. Can she pitch in AA or AAA? No. Maybe one day." Women had proven in the last quarter of the century they could do anything a man could do, but baseball still was a male-dominated world, and it didn't look as if Borders was going to change it. Maybe one day, but most of the men doubted it.

Borders moved on to Madison, Wisconsin, in the Northern League, where she got better. In 1999 she led the Black Wolf pitching staff with a 1.67 earned run average in thirty-two and a third innings. That's outstanding, reminiscent of the time when she struck out all eighteen boys she faced in a Little League game. She eventually pitched for the baseball team at Whittier College in California but wasn't well received by the opposing men. In eleven times at bat, she was hit by pitches eleven times.

She started the 2000 season with the Black Wolf but hadn't played in any games when she asked for her release on June 9. She was picked up by the Zion Pioneerzz of Saint George, Utah, and played the rest of the month in the Western Baseball League. In eight and two-thirds innings over five games, she had a 9.35 ERA. On June 29, after giving up three runs with what she thought was her best stuff against the Feather River Mudcats, she retired at age twenty-six. Borders knew she had given baseball all the time she could. "I happen to think it's pretty fantastic that I'm the only female to ever play baseball with the guys. I wasn't out to prove women's rights or anything. I love baseball," Borders said. One of her many uniforms now hangs in the Baseball Hall of Fame.

I don't know whether it was the novelty of seeing Borders pitch and the electrified crowd or just the entertaining level of baseball in the Northern League, but it was fun being at the ballpark with my son, the way I always dreamed it should be. The Dukes had a few low-key contests and some music between innings, but the focus still was on the game, unlike Saint Paul where the game seemed to resemble a TV game show. In fact, more than once the Saints played the theme song for *The Price Is Right* while

I waited for Bob Barker to tell me to come on down. Jerad, my younger son, Matthew, my wife, Lynn, and I had been to many Cavaliers games in Eau Claire, and the boys usually wanted to leave by midgame, unless prizes were to be awarded. The Dukes game kept Jerad's interest, as I'm sure the Saints game would have. "This is actually fun," he said, and then I realized that he never saw baseball as fun, that he never saw a game where the crowd and the teams were intense. That included several Twins games at the Metrodome. He previously thought baseball was boring. In Duluth, he ate cotton candy, soda, and popcorn and paid attention for nine innings. When I pointed out, from our third-base side seats, strategical moves by the managers, he listened and watched. By mid-game he was asking many questions about baseball—how pitchers throw a changeup, who invented the game, and what was the longest game ever. I felt a little closer to him as we walked through the parking lot, the halo of Wade Stadium hovering over us, the cool night air beginning to blow in off Lake Superior.

As much as I was distracted from baseball at the Saints game, I had to admit that the excitement for baseball in the new Northern League was impressive. The level of baseball was good. The fans were having fun. I was wishing we had a team in Eau Claire.

We drove west through the dark on Minnesota Highway 2 and talked about the game until Jerad dozed off. Night driving either puts you to sleep or gives you a lot of time to think about things, like Iowa and corn. I knew that just to our north was Chisholm, Minnesota, where Archibald "Moonlight" Graham practiced medicine, died, and then became famous in the baseball fantasy movie *Field of Dreams* for posthumously getting his chance to bat against a Major League pitcher. Earlier that summer we visited the Field of Dreams, near Dyersville, Iowa, where the movie was filmed, and Jerad hit a ball into the now-famous corn field. We also attended a family reunion in nearby Sumner, Iowa, visiting with relatives and the descendants of relatives who had spent their lives growing corn. Iowa is corn, and for my ancestors corn is a symbol of home. Sitting on picnic tables in a city park shelter, the reunionists sang with pride a song's crescendo refrain, "Iowa, Iowa—that's where the tall! corn!! grows!!!" Among the singers were my father, John, and my mother, Edna, and aunts and uncles, all descendants of northern European immigrants who settled the Midwest a century and a half earlier. My parents had met in down-town Sumner one summer evening fifty-eight years earlier. Soon they left the farm, left Iowa, and raised seven children in Eau Claire, Wisconsin, none of them farmers. After the reunion we visited the farm where my father had been a hired hand. Then we stopped at another farm where my mother used to watch her father, Bernard Flanscha, plant the straightest corn rows in Fayette County, according to her. She stood near that same field, again full of corn, as I snapped her photo. The farm with its long, long driveway had changed some, she said, but the corn rows hadn't. As we left Iowa behind and returned to Wisconsin, another song caught my attention. "It's good to touch the green, green grass of home," the senti-mental baritone voice of Roger Whittaker crooned over the radio. I looked in the rearview mirror, and my mother had a faraway look in her eye. We had just touched the green grass of her home, maybe for the last time in her life. I doubt she ever played baseball or played catch with her father or siblings back in the 1920s and 1930s. She probably had heard of Babe Ruth but didn't follow pro baseball during one of its golden eras. Standing on the grass of home, she was thinking about her father, about her childhood. I knew then why the baseball movie was popular. Everybody wants to go home one more time, to be with their father or mother or to be young enough, or young enough at heart, to dream again. Baseball, at its core, is all about getting another chance to go home, to go where you belong. We see that every time a player safely crosses home plate, is welcomed by his baseball family, and returns to the shaded shelter of the dugout. We see it, and it makes us glad.

NORTH TO CLEARBROOK, MINNESOTA

We were going away from home. After spending the night in Grand Rapids, Minnesota, where *Wizard of Oz* actress Judy Garland was born, we followed a blacktop road through the Chippewa National Forest. Like the lion in Oz, the minor league ballplayers who crossed this lonely part of Minnesota surely were searching for their hearts in the forest. Was baseball worth all this? En route, we passed the hamlet of Ballclub, Min-nesota. The only store in town sold gas, liquor, and groceries. A woman inside told me that the town's name had nothing to do with baseball. The name came from Native Americans who invented their own game, lacrosse, with a ball and a club. We were passing through the Leech Lake Indian Reservation.

We passed Bemidji, Minnesota, the hockey haven and home of a Paul Bunyan and Babe the Blue Ox statue, and turned north off Highway 2 onto Highway 5. Rain was falling as we pulled up to the front door of the Wes Westrum Baseball Museum on Main Street in Clearbrook, Minnesota. We were a bit late, and Westrum was waiting for us at the front door, as an old-time baseball manager would. Luckily, he didn't fine us or make us run laps.

Westrum was used to waiting. He signed his first pro contract in 1939 at age sixteen with the Grand Forks Chiefs, but his mother voided it because she said he was too young. He played for Crookston, Minnesota, in 1940 and the Eau Claire Bears in 1941 at age eighteen, hitting .330. It would be another six years before he made the majors, mostly because he spent three years in World War II. The Giants finally called him up

Wes Westrum, at the Wes Westrum Museum in Clearbrook, Minnesota, retired in his hometown after a long pro baseball career that took him from the Eau Claire Bears to the New York Giants.

(Photo by Jerry Poling)

in 1947, and he played his first game on the road at Chicago's Wrigley Field, the same place where ten years earlier he had seen his first Major League game and said to himself, "Someday I'll be back."

In eleven seasons with the New York Giants he was a National League All-Star two times, in 1952 and 1953. Experts consider Westrum one of the greatest catchers of one of baseball's golden eras. In 1950 he set a record for catchers by committing only one error, and he shouldn't have been charged with that, he said, because he threw to second base on a steal and no one was covering as the ball flew into center field. No mistakes in 140 games. That year was his best offensively too as he hit twenty-three home runs. Although he had only a .217 lifetime batting average, he ranks third among the great catchers in on-base percentage, ahead of such better-known backstops as Yogi Berra, Thurman Munson, Johnny Bench, and Carlton Fisk. And this was despite the fact he suffered eight broken fingers in his career, making it hard to hold a bat. But he didn't get any sympathy from Giants manager Leo Durocher. When he broke a finger, Durocher would tell him to tape it and rub the finger in the dirt so the opponents wouldn't notice. After he retired, Westrum managed the New York Mets from 1965 to 1967 and the San Francisco Giants in 1974 and 1975.

For thirty years he lived the life of pro baseball royalty. Now here he was at age seventy-five, retired near this north central Minnesota town where he grew up. Much like Burleigh Grimes, he had come home for his final years and was happy just to be a hometown hero. He still gets ten to twelve autograph requests in the mail each week from fans around the country. As he showed Jerad and me around his shrine in an American Legion hall, three young softball players came in. They were in a district tournament in Clearbrook and had heard about the museum. They said to Westrum, Jerad, and me, "Who is this Wes Westrum guy?" I took the liberty to introduce them to a smiling Wes, and soon the congenial Westrum was giving autographs and telling them old jokes like, "You're the salt of the earth. I've been trying to shake you a long time." It was easy to see where his life had gone; he felt at ease around people who knew how to play ball.

The museum was devoted to Westrum's memorabilia—balls and bats signed by Hall of Famers, his old uniforms, and news clippings. Many items still were in storage, and he reportedly has a personal shrine of treasured items. Over in one corner of the museum was a mural of "The

Catch." Willie Mays made what is considered the greatest catch in base-ball history in game one of the 1954 World Series against the Cleveland Indians, running straight toward the center field wall and snaring the ball over his shoulder. Westrum had the best view in the house—he was playing catcher for the Giants. Westrum didn't dispute the greatness of the catch or Mays's amazing abilities, but he said the mural and historians' memory of the catch was off: Mays was more to right center field—not dead center—when he pulled it in. Westrum caught all four games of the Series as the Giants swept the Indians.

Although Westrum didn't make baseball history, he had a knack for being around it. Westrum witnessed another of baseball's greatest moments in 1951 when teammate Bobby Thomson hit the dramatic home run that gave the Giants the pennant over the Brooklyn Dodgers. Thomson's hit drove in Clint Hartung from third base and sailed over the head of Dodgers left fielder Andy Pafko. Hartung and Pafko were also Eau Claire stars from the 1940s. But Westrum did make journalism history by appearing on the cover of the debut issue of *Sports Illustrated* on August 16, 1954. The cover photo shows Westrum catching, the Milwaukee Braves' Eddie Mathews at bat, and umpire Augie Donatelli behind the plate at Milwaukee County Stadium. The issue is a collector's item now, and one is on display at the Wes Westrum Hall of Fame in Clearbrook.

Westrum grew up in virtually all-white northern Minnesota, but he didn't have any trouble adjusting to blacks in the Major Leagues, possibly because he began playing in 1947, the same year that Jackie Robinson broke the color barrier. In fact, Westrum said his best friends in base-ball were black: Willie Mays, Willie McCovey, Monte Irvin, and Henry Aaron. In the late 1970s, his managing career finished, Westrum sought out Aaron—who then was Atlanta Braves minor league director—and was given a job as an advance game scout. They had become friends over the years. "He was a good fella. He had the best pair of wrists I ever saw," Westrum said of Aaron. Wes Westrum passed away May 28, 2002.

FLAT OUT TO FARGO

After Clearbrook we hit the road again. Farther along Highway 2 to the west was Grand Forks, North Dakota. In 1952 Aaron and the Eau Claire Bears spent the last five days of July on the road, playing three games in

Grand Forks—where Aaron hit a three-run homer—and three in Fargo—where he went 0-for-11 and began the late-season slide that cost him the batting title. Grand Forks didn't have a team now, so we headed south and west toward Fargo. In just a hop or a jump we would be across the Mississippi River and there. Jerad lobbied to stop at Lake Itasca State Park, headwaters of the Mississippi. Thousands of tourists come each year to see the trickle of water at one end of the lake that eventually turns into the Mississippi River. I took Jerad's photo next to the sign: "Here 1,475 feet above the ocean the mighty Mississippi begins to flow on its winding way 2,552 miles to the Gulf of Mexico." Henry Aaron grew up on the Gulf of Mexico in Mobile, and the sign reminded me of the long road he had taken—much longer than midwesterners Westrum, Maris, Grimes, or Pafko—to break into the minor leagues when he was just a teenager. Aaron must have been mentally mature to focus on his goal of succeeding in baseball despite the continental divide in distance and culture. I remember Aaron saying that he had no trouble sleeping on the road, waking up ready to play when the Bears reached the outposts of the Northern League. He was no tourist.

Many consecutive days on the road would get old quickly—especially in a car full of shower-deprived, flatulent ballplayers—but Jerad and I knew we had only a few hours between stops so we made the most of them, grabbing snacks and sodas for the ride and watching the scenery. We also listened to Minnesota Public Radio, which amused us with a half hour program on the merits of composting by using worms. The only drawback, we were told, was the worm juice that collected at the bottom of the bin and had to be dumped occasionally. Next, an MPR guest offered tips on matching wines with fast foods, a hearty red with a Big Mac, a subtle white with Kentucky Fried Chicken. We were swigging cream soda and laughing so much that we didn't pay attention to the next guest, who probably was an expert at breads that go down well after eating lutefisk, the infamous lye-bathed fish that needs a bread chaser to prevent backwash. No wonder Garrison Keillor never runs out of material for *Prairie Home Companion*; he listens to MPR. The station gradually faded out, and we had to stop anyway on some dirt road in the brush to relieve ourselves of cream soda, which had complemented our fast food beautifully.

The road finally had put Jerad to sleep again. The lakes, spruce, and pine trees of north central Minnesota gradually gave way to the rolling wheat fields and ever-flatter landscape of the western Minnesota prairie. North Dakota is more famous for its agricultural plants than its people, Roger Maris and blues singer Johnny Lang notwithstanding. The state has less tree cover (2 percent) than any other state in the union. As we approached Fargo, we were driving on an ancient lake bed, the silt of which now is among the most fertile farming regions in the nation. The prairies are known for producing durum wheat, which is turned into the pasta that feeds many a carbohydrate-conscious athlete. North Dakota also produces half the nation's sunflower seeds, the shells of which are spit out by many an anxious pro baseball player.

Just northwest of Fargo is Cooperstown, North Dakota. I wondered if Northern League players who dreamed of making the Baseball Hall of Fame in Cooperstown, New York, ever knew that another Cooperstown existed and that it signified not how far they had come but how far they had to go. Most likely, the players who never made it out of the Northern League told their friends years later that they almost made it to Cooperstown.

As we approached Moorhead, the sister city of Fargo (the original Twins, by the way, weren't the Minnesota Twins but the Fargo-Moorhead Twins), Jerad awoke to the almost surrealistic tabletop landscape, uninterrupted views as long as five miles we guessed, of nothing but farmland. Was this where the young Aaron awoke and began to see the limitless possibilities of his baseball career? Fargo was, after all, where Aaron hit his first professional home run against a white pitcher. Is it coincidence that Aaron and Maris, who broke Babe Ruth's most hallowed records, can trace their home run roots to a land with no visual limits? Fargo, after all, is named after a man whose life was built on going places fast. George William Fargo helped start Wells, Fargo and Company, which was famous for its express stagecoach runs to the West during the gold rush days of the middle 1800s.

On a celluloid trip through the Eau Claire *Leader* I had discovered that, aside from the fact that Maris was able to play minor league ball in his hometown while Aaron played 2,552 Mississippi River miles away from home, they had a lot in common. The blue-plastic microfilm wheel spun faster and faster as it carried me further into the past. Time was flying by. I cut the engine. It was 1953. The headlines of June 2 drifted into view. "Britain Crowns Queen Elizabeth II." "Ike Blocks Cutoff on Funds for UN." "Korea Will Cooperate with Yanks." On the sports page was the banner, "Fargo-Moorhead Overtakes Bears 5–3," over a report of a baseball game the night before seen by 666 fans in Eau Claire. In the fifth paragraph, there it was: "[Lynn] Southworth, who took his second loss against no wins, pitched creditably and had a one-hitter going into the seventh and a 3–0 lead. Rog Maras' second inning double was Southworth's only hit given up."

The old spelling of the Maris name with an *a* instead of an *i* threw me momentarily, but I knew it was a reference to the first-ever at bat at Carson Park by one of baseball's now-immortal players. Just eight years later, Maris hit sixty-one home runs in 1961 to break Babe Ruth's coveted season record. As I stared at the microfilm, I couldn't help but think that fifty weeks earlier on that same Carson Park field, Henry Aaron collected his first pro hit on his way toward breaking the other famous Ruth record, that of 714 career homers.

One was black, one white. One was from the South, one from the North. But Aaron and Maris are indelibly linked. Both began their pro baseball careers in the Class C Northern League at age eighteen. Neither was a home run hitter. Both had the same inauspicious total of nine home

Fargo-Moorhead standout Roger Maris played in the Northern League in 1953, one year after Henry Aaron. Both players went on to break home run records set by Babe Ruth.

(Photo courtesy of Roger Maris Museum, Fargo, North Dakota)

runs in their first Northern League seasons, giving no indication that one day they would surpass the Sultan of Swat. Aaron hit his first pro home run in 1952 in Maris's hometown. That summer in the same stadium, old Barnett Field, Maris was hitting homers for the Moorhead Chicks, a local amateur team. Maybe Maris saw Aaron play that year in Fargo. Aaron and Maris were soft-spoken anti-Ruths, shying away from attention and ignoring occasional taunts that they didn't deserve to beat the Babe's marks. Both were outstanding right fielders when they surpassed Ruth, another right fielder. Both were born in 1934, when Ruth was in his last full season. Maris wound up playing nine games at Carson Park in 1953 on four road trips to Eau Claire. He didn't hit a homer at Carson Park, but he didn't have to. His team dominated the Northern League behind a thirty-year-old with thick glasses named Frank Gravino, who hit a league record and a Ruth-like fifty-two homers in 126 games and was the league's Most Valuable Player. Maris hit .325 for the 1953 season; Aaron had hit .336 the year before. Aaron was the 1952 Northern League Rookie of the Year, and Maris was the top rookie in 1953.

Maris was born in Hibbing, Minnesota, and grew up in Grand Forks and Fargo. His given surname was Maras, but baseball and his father changed that. Apparently while in the minor leagues in 1953 or 1954 in Keokuk, Iowa, some opposing fans began to verbally add a second *s* to the end of Maras's name, changed the emphasis to the second syllable, and taunted him with the insinuating pronunciation, *Mare-ass*. "So the father [Rudy Maras], kind of a feisty guy, changed the name to Maris. He thought it was uncalled for," said Jim McLaughlin, curator of the Roger Maris Museum in Fargo. One of the largest pieces of memorabilia in the Maris museum is a 1953 Northern League pennant. The most important, however, is the ball Maris hit for his record-tying sixtieth home run. The sixty-first home run ball is in the Baseball Hall of Fame.

Baseball in Fargo isn't what it used to be. It's much better. Maris played in old Barnett Field in Fargo, now the site of a high school. The new Northern League Fargo Redhawks play in a modern $6 million stadium that probably would have cost $10 million if community leaders hadn't chipped in. Newman Outdoor Field has theater-style box seats, a mezzanine, luxury suites, a hot tub for fans, a playground for kids, and room for forty-five hundred people. They should have made the stadium bigger. It was Fan Appreciation Night, and the second-largest crowd in history,

6,369, was on hand for the game against the Sioux Falls Canaries. It didn't hurt that the Redhawks were the best team in the league, on their way to a 64-21 record and a 3-0 sweep of the Saints in the championship series. Not everyone was into the Redhawks. On the way to the game, we stopped at a Fargo gas station to ask directions. The young woman at the counter had no idea what we were talking about. She had never heard of the stadium or the baseball team. After we left the station, the woman probably was saying the same thing the irreverent Saint Paul Saints announcer said: "Whatever."

This still was a 1990s version of minor league baseball, but the Redhawks, like the Duluth-Superior Dukes, kept the focus on the game. The Redhawks' ballboys were middle-aged men in farmers' bib overalls named Sven and Ole. They sat on the sidelines in rocking chairs. Down the foul lines balls were chased by attractive young blonde women (granddaughters of Scandinavian immigrants, no doubt) in white shorts and red shirts. Afterward, fans saw a twenty-minute pyrotechnics show, with sulfur-fueled sparks shooting in home run arcs from beyond the outfield fence. But marketing didn't upstage history altogether. In centerfield was Maris's 1953 Fargo-Moorhead number 8. It was retired in a ceremony two months earlier. Too bad somebody rich financed the stadium. It should have been named Maris Stadium instead of Newman Outdoor Field.

After a day on the road, Jerad and I enjoyed the comfort of a glassed-in, climate-controlled, carpeted press box, easily more roomy and modern than the one at Milwaukee County Stadium. Media life was beginning to appeal to Jerad after his third free soda and fourth bag of snack chips, and I didn't mind so much when a thunderstorm rolled in from the prairie and halted the game. We stayed dry and got to talk with Maury Wills, a Maris contemporary, one of the greatest base stealers in baseball history and now a color commentator on Redhawks radio broadcasts. He is a big fan of the Northern League. "We've got some teams that could play in AAA, like the Redhawks and Winnipeg, and players throughout the league that can play Major League ball. I think it's an outstanding league."

Wills knew all about paying dues in the minor leagues. He spent eight and a half years in the Dodgers minor leagues and recalled twenty-two-hour bus trips. When he finally reached the majors, everyone noticed. He was the National League MVP in 1962—the year after Maris hit sixty one home runs—when he stole 104 bases and broke Ty Cobb's record. He was a seven-time National League All-Star. In 1980 he accomplished what Aaron had been pushing for a long time. Wills was named manager of the Seattle Mariners. Only two other blacks before him, Frank Robinson and Larry Doby, had been Major League managers. Wills also has coached in various positions in the majors ever since. Wills was at his base-stealing best when Aaron was hitting most of his home runs in the 1960s, but he said Aaron was a superstar because he had five weapons. "Aaron could run, throw, field, hit, and hit with power. Mays, Frank Robinson—only a few others could do all five. A lot of superstars today can only do two."

The rain let up, and the Redhawks won. In the locker room a five-feet-nine, 200-pound ball of muscle, Darryl Motley, was dressing slowly. At age thirty-nine, he was in his twentieth and final year of pro baseball, having played in more than twenty-seven hundred games. It was his third year with Fargo-Moorhead, and even though he had played parts of seven Major League seasons in Kansas City and Atlanta, even though he hit a seventh-game home run that gave the Royals the 1985 World Series title, he still was getting nervous before games in the Northern League. "It's my love of the game," he said. His attitude toward baseball was one that players from the old Northern League, like Aaron and Maris, could understand.

The next morning we talked to one of Maris's boyhood friends and saw the Roger Maris Museum at the West Acres Shopping Mall. Maris was buried in Fargo in 1985 after dying of cancer, and the feeling around the town of seventy-five thousand was funereal again because McGwire and Sosa were ready to break his home run record. The Maris mystique—the inscription on his headstone is "Against All Odds"—didn't seem quite so magical now that others could copy him. Don Gooselaw, a pallbearer at Maris's funeral, remembers he was playing softball in Fargo on the afternoon of Sunday, October 1, 1961, when he heard the radio announcement that Maris had hit number sixty-one. Three weeks after I talked to Gooselaw, McGwire hit number sixty-two. "I think maybe now [Maris] will get his due and get elected to the Hall of Fame," Gooselaw said. Maris himself had mentioned to friends before he died that he already was being forgotten by baseball fans. Not at the museum. A short but continuous line of people filed past the Maris memorabilia. James McLaughlin, one of the founders of the museum and its curator, knows how important the memory of Maris is to Fargoans and others. "One man in his eighties made a special trip here from Chicago to see the museum. I gave him a card signed by Maris. He cried on the spot."

Jerad and I watched the flat land begin to roll again as we started our 350-mile trip back to Eau Claire. We took a rest stop in Saint Cloud, Minnesota. In 1952 the Eau Claire Bears played nine games in Saint Cloud against the Rox. The city didn't have a new Northern League team, but it did have the Minnesota Baseball Hall of Fame Museum. We stopped and learned that more than twenty-four men in the Baseball Hall of Fame were from Minnesota or played for a Minnesota team, including Ted Williams and Willie Mays. We got back on the road, but the legend of Willie seemed to have followed us from the Wes Westrum museum in Clearbrook. We were listening to the broadcast of the Twins game, and Minnesota native Paul Molitor collected career hit 3,283, tying him for ninth on the all-time hit list with Mays. In 1951 Mays was with the Minneapolis Millers when he was called up to the majors by the New York Giants.

The museum helped bring our trip into focus. We talked about athletes who devoted their lives to their sport. For decades, young men of all athletic abilities—from town team players to future Hall of Famers—had crossed these Wisconsin, Minnesota, and Dakota hills, prairies, and rivers because baseball was their passion. They weren't the first. These baseball men were just the latest in a parade of passionate people seeking midwestern magic. They included Negro League pitching legend Satchel Paige. On a 108-degree day in July of 1935, Paige pitched one inning for the Bismarck All-Stars when they defeated the Rapid City All-Stars. Players like Paige, even as great as they were, often jumped from one team to another year after year, several times a year or even from one week to the next to eke out a living. Among them was Buck O'Neil, another Negro Leaguer who barnstormed west of the Mississippi in the 1930s and 1940s. O'Neil kept a book that listed homes where black players would be accepted for the night when they finished a game. The Negro Leaguers were playing in the sparsely populated, agricultural land of the Northern League—North and South Dakota, Minnesota, Manitoba—but were castoffs there as in the South. O'Neil never made the Baseball Hall of Fame, like Paige did, but he did become the first black coach in the majors, as an assistant with the Chicago Cubs beginning in 1962.

Among the thousands of other people who had hope when they came to this land, three others come to mind. In 1861 Henry David Thoreau, the author of *Walden,* came west to Minnesota because he was dying of tuberculosis and needed fresh air. He traveled by steamboat up the Mississippi, studied the stems and petals of native prairie plants, met with Native Americans, and was invigorated. He was forty-three and died less than a year later. In 1878 Wisconsin native Hamlin Garland traveled west by train through Minnesota to Ordway, South Dakota, to stake a claim. In the middle to late 1800s, midwestern lands were flooded by immigrants—mostly from northern Europe—trying to prove themselves on the undisturbed grasslands that Thoreau had so delighted in. Intimidated by the fierce blizzards, Garland soon gave up sodbusting and wrote about the back-breaking hardships of homesteading and the headstrong pioneers who were hell-bent on succeeding in the harsh environment. He won a Pulitzer Prize; like Aaron, he succeeded after a soul-searching experience helped him mature and move on. In 1920 Sinclair Lewis published the quintessential American novel *Main Street,* which chronicled life in the Midwest, ostensibly in his hometown of Sauk Centre, Minnesota, near Saint Cloud. He wrote about the kinds of people who had taken root in the small cities to pursue their American dreams. Those aging *Main Street* people and their descendants were the ones who provided Aaron with images of life in Middle America on his way to becoming a mainstream cultural icon fifty years later.

On the way home, I realized that the sometimes harsh land of the Northern League has a long history of dreams lost and found, of people trying to prove themselves on a cleared piece of prairie, be it farm, city lot, or baseball field. Wisconsin, Minnesota, and the Dakotas were Henry Aaron's proving grounds in 1952. They were fair; some of the whitest states in the Union gave a young black man reason to keep dreaming. Aaron came to the Midwest for many of the same reasons as the immigrants, drawn by equal opportunity, undaunted by obstacles. He was up to the challenge.

chapter 4

STATUESQUE

Aaron's return for the statue dedication at Carson Park in 1994 was his third visit to Eau Claire after he left in 1952.

His first return visit was for a banquet on January 23, 1962, with Milwaukee Braves teammate Joe Torre. By then, Aaron was a national baseball hero. Two days earlier he and teammate Eddie Mathews had signed new contracts. Aaron was twenty-seven and coming off a season in which he hit .327, slugged 34 home runs, and batted in 120 runs. More than 250 baseball fans paid three dollars each to attend the annual Eau Claire Braves kickoff dinner at the Hotel Eau Claire, the same place where Aaron had considered quitting baseball ten years earlier. Not only were Aaron and Torre on hand, but the Braves sent team president John McHale, farm system director John Mullen, and publicity director Donald Davidson.

Eau Claire had such a strong baseball tradition that it even had its own baseball hall of fame. That night Aaron's 1952 coach, Bill Adair, was added to the shrine, joining Wes Westrum, Andy Pafko, Henry Majeski, Andy Cohen, Jim Delsing, team founder Herman White, Billy Bruton, and Aaron. When asked that night what he remembered about his minor league debut in Eau Claire, Aaron recalled that he had thirty-five errors at shortstop (an average of almost one every other game). "We needed a taller first baseman," he joked. He probably didn't remember that Dick Engquist, the Bears' first baseman that year, was six-feet-four.

During that trip to Eau Claire, Aaron and Torre drove thirty miles west to the nearby town of Durand, Wisconsin, to visit Emma Brion. For forty-nine years, the sixty-three-year-old Brion had been bedridden, the result of complications from a surgery when she was a teenager. Aaron gave her an autographed baseball, and someone took a photo of the two men in winter overcoats standing at her bedside, Brion flat on her back looking up at them. Before she died in 1975, less than a year after Aaron broke Babe Ruth's record and after spending sixty-one years in bed, she called the visit from Aaron—her hero—the high point of her life.

Aaron was scheduled to return to Eau Claire in September of 1981 to give a speech and make appearances but abruptly canceled with little or no explanation. Some people thought he was just another wealthy athlete who had grown too big for his roots. Some thought he had forgotten about Eau Claire. Aaron did finally return in 1982 to give a speech at the University of Wisconsin–Eau Claire and meet with some old Bears friends, and one of the first things he said to the audience was, "I'd like to apologize for not being here last year. There were some things that happened that were beyond my control. I hope that I'm forgiven for that." Unfortunately, the apology was not acknowledged in a newspaper story the next day so most people in the city never heard it. In 1994 many city residents recalled 1981 and remained skeptical about whether or not Aaron actually would arrive for the statue dedication.

His eighteen-minute speech in 1982, "The Courage to Succeed," barely mentioned baseball, even though he had been elected to the Baseball Hall of Fame only two weeks earlier along with another black star, Frank Robinson. In 1982 Aaron was more than a baseball player and certainly not the shy eighteen-year-old of 1952. He was a statesmanlike crusader for children, equality in society, and black civil rights, telling the thousand people in attendance that Americans need to change the way they think. He raised issues like those fought for by Martin Luther King Jr., and he quoted Shakespeare and Socrates. "The motivation to make the world a better place to live will not be found in textbooks. It can only be found in you. If you are to make the universe better, you are to make *your* universe better. When good people refuse to stand up, bad people will." He cited the rise of Hitler and the tragedy of African slave trade. "Slavery in America endured for centuries until Americans had the courage to end it. Needless oppression ... knows no time, no place, color, or limitation to the extent any human being is rejected, denied opportunity because of his or her religion, held in contempt because of his or her sex. To that extent, all of us are victims. It is an awesome task we face, putting our society back together. You will discover in time that the challenge comes not nearly so much from without as it does from within. There comes a time when those who know better must always do better."

Aaron read from his notes and didn't command the crowd as Martin Luther King Jr. could, but his message sounded somewhat like King's. In 1963, in his famous "Letter from Birmingham Jail," King wrote about the "appalling silence of good people" and the need for individuals to stand up to injustice: "We must use time creatively, in the knowledge that the time is always ripe to do right."

In March 1962, two months after Aaron's visit, King also went to Eau Claire. "Ol' Man Segregation is on his deathbed," King told a large crowd at the university, according to the *Daily Telegram*. "The walls of racial seg-regation are gradually crumbling," helped along by a nonviolent means of revolution that "will so appeal to your heart and conscience that we will not only win our just rights but win you too." King asked President Kennedy to issue a second Emancipation Proclamation and declare segre-gation unconstitutional. "The South has long tried to live in monologue instead of dialogue," he said. The audience gave King a standing ovation. In the audience was John S. Schneider, a retired history and sociology professor who for years had longed to see and hear King. Minutes after King's speech, Schneider was leaving the auditorium when he collapsed and died of a heart attack in the arms of two friends.

King's visit to Eau Claire has long been forgotten. No audio or visual record of the speech exists, and few people are aware that King visited, let alone just one year before his seminal "I Have a Dream" speech in Wash-ington. But the people of Eau Claire remember their own black hero, Aaron. The University of Wisconsin–Eau Claire started a scholarship fund for minority students in Aaron's name. In 1994 Aaron established the national Chasing the Dream Foundation to enable children ages nine to twelve to pursue instruction in the arts.

Aaron's 1982 return to Eau Claire was subdued compared to his return in 1994. The groundwork for Aaron's return was laid in 1993 when a Henry Aaron Tribute committee of city residents formed. They worked a year and a half on the statue project and raised nearly twenty thousand dollars from businesses and individuals. The city council unanimously approved plans to locate the Aaron statue on city land.

Given that the stadium and park complex is the most used and most visible public gathering place in the city, the council's vote was significant. The city had helped one of the nation's most famous people get his start, and it was proud to recognize that. The council made the concession with the stipulation that all money for the statue would be raised privately. Eventually, the city committed some money for the ceremony and to install and maintain the statue. Few people said anything negative about the statue, although some grumbled that other people, namely team founder and steward Herman White, who kept the team together for decades, had done far more for city baseball than Aaron. They were right. White owned a small manufacturing company and was also city council president during the early 1950s. White did more in the long run than Aaron, but the few naysayers didn't realize that Aaron symbolized everything White had worked for—recognition for Eau Claire baseball and for the city. What more could the city ask for than a chance to call Henry Aaron its own? Even Herman White would have been proud to know that one of baseball's greatest ever came from his humble Class C team.

Most important, Aaron was proud that Eau Claire wanted him to be part of city heritage. Flying in alone from Atlanta that morning, he knew that he would give two speeches, unveil the statue, and hold a news conference. But he didn't know what type of reception to expect. Aaron wasn't even sure if Carson Park stadium was still standing. He missed his direct flight from Atlanta to Minneapolis because the plane left ten minutes early, leaving him standing in the Atlanta terminal and wondering how to get to Eau Claire. He found a seat on another plane, which first stopped in Jacksonville, Florida, the only other city where he played minor league ball. By the time he arrived in Eau Claire, Aaron had traced his pre–Major League path in reverse order: Georgia for spring training in 1954, Jacksonville in 1953, and Eau Claire in 1952. Each stop on August 17, 1994, took him further back in time chronologically. When he reached Eau Claire, he must have thought he'd stepped off a time machine. He had gone back to his beginning.

Although he was sixty years old and known the world over, in some ways he was still the teenager who played in Eau Claire and was looking for respect. People idolized Babe Ruth, not Aaron, even though Aaron had led a far more exemplary life. He still expressed publicly the deep hurt he experienced in 1974 when some fans saw him as less of a man than Ruth because he was black, and he was still criticized for speaking out about it.

Aaron signed autograph after autograph in Eau Claire, so many that he wound up missing his scheduled flight home that night. Officials at the dedication had been warned that he might not be an approachable person, was quiet, sometimes moody, didn't sign autographs, and might not be a crowd pleaser. In fact, he might not even show up, said those who remembered 1981. But Aaron was just the opposite of his alleged persona—warm, helpful, conscientious, and outgoing.

After a luncheon speech, his first task was to reveal the life-size bronze bust of himself as a lean eighteen-year-old Bear, holding a bat on his right shoulder, his head held high and his eye on the future. When the veil dropped, Aaron admired it for several minutes, waved to the cheering

Henry Aaron drew a large crowd to Eau Claire in 1994 when he returned to Carson Park for the unveiling of a bronze bust in his honor. The bust depicts Aaron as an eighteen-year-old shortstop for the Eau Claire Bears.

(Dan Reiland photo, courtesy of the *Eau Claire Leader-Telegram*)

crowd, and said privately to organizers around him that it made him proud. He thanked the sculptor's wife.

The sculptor, Ken Campbell, had died after open-heart surgery only weeks after he and his wife, Jane, delivered the clay Aaron to a foundry in Utah. Both in their sixties, the Campbells had transferred the statue from their studio to a van, secured it against shifting, and headed more than a thousand miles cross-country. For the first time in forty-two years, a young Henry Aaron was traveling across the Midwest again with a bat on his shoulder.

Campbell was a longtime Eau Claire resident, a university art professor, and an international expert on African art. His house was a museum of African masks and other tribal art. When the idea of honoring Aaron began to circulate in Eau Claire, Campbell was the first to propose a statue. He couldn't wait to get his hands on clay again, especially for a chance to portray one of the leading black figures of the twentieth century in the United States. Earlier Campbell had created Eau Claire's statue of Old Abe, a bald eagle that followed the Eighth Wisconsin Regiment into battle during the Civil War.

Most proud of his five works in the American Indian Hall of Fame in Anadarko, Oklahoma, Campbell became equally proud of his Aaron sculpture as the clay likeness slowly took shape in his studio during the spring of 1994. He used wood heat to make the clay pliable on cold Wisconsin mornings, when he and Jane, also an artist, daily greeted the emerging figure, "Good morning, Mr. Aaron."

Campbell was losing his eyesight to glaucoma and his life to a bad heart on the days he breathed life once again into young Henry Aaron. Function followed form as he built a human being from the inside out, starting with a rib-cage armature made of chicken wire fastened to wood. Then he applied layers of clay for the organs, bones, muscles, skin, and hair. Campbell didn't have the luxury of a sitting with Aaron before he began work on the statue. He measured Aaron's bust using only photos of him as a young man. Campbell was dying, but he was making sure the legend of Henry Aaron never would pass away in Eau Claire.

After the unveiling, Aaron was feted in the stadium—contrary to the report of one sportswriter. A Minnesota Twins beat writer from the Twin

Cities—assigned to cover the dedication of Aaron's statue while the Major Leagues were on strike—departed after the unveiling and later wrote that Aaron flew home to Atlanta without saying a word of thanks in public in Eau Claire. While Aaron did not say anything publicly at the unveiling, he did give a speech at the stadium, an event the writer missed completely. Despite many letters of protest proving the story wrong, the writer did not fully retract his incorrect, negative depiction of Aaron's efforts but simply wrote a brief addendum the next day. His was the only story about the event that made the national sports wires, although an accurate Associated Press story went out to Wisconsin media. Twenty years after receiving hate mail while breaking Ruth's record, people still were ready to criticize Aaron at the least opportunity or none at all. On a day when he went out of his way to please the crowds and the organizers, at least one person still saw him as an angry, victimized black man who wasn't through fighting. After his bittersweet baseball experience ended in 1976, Aaron began to speak about what was right and wrong with the game rather than worry about his image. When he criticized the institution of baseball for giving few opportunities to blacks beyond the playing field, he often was portrayed as ungrateful rather than as a reformer.

As the misguided sportswriter drove home, the real festivities began. Aaron got back in the limousine and entered the stadium through a center field gate. The event was predictably choreographed, but for a sometimes sleepy city like Eau Claire, most people with their cameras, camcorders, baseballs, and memories thought it was the most exciting city spectacle in many years. People were excited to see Aaron, and Aaron appeared excited to be there. The city council president proclaimed Henry Aaron Day, hundreds of residents signed a giant greeting card, and officials made speeches. Aaron dabbed his eyes during the national anthem and gave a thoughtful speech about the value of education over home runs and the importance of helping children in America. This was the man who left high school early to pursue a baseball dream but later finished his high school requirements and received his diploma. Players waiting to take the field for the CABA World Series stood at attention in front of the dugouts, their eyes riveted on one of the greatest ever to play the game they love.

Standing near the pitching mound, Aaron impressed the crowd with words that went far beyond baseball:

So often, when you think about Hank Aaron, everyone thinks in terms of home runs. Someone asked me just this afternoon how would I like to be remembered. I suppose I want to be remembered for breaking Babe Ruth's record, but that's not the greatest thing in the world. The greatest thing I would like to be remembered for is the fact that I've worked for many years for Big Brothers and Big Sisters, and I've said this many times that the greatest commodity we have is our children. I was extremely lucky to have played baseball for twenty-three years. Home runs is something that I've put on a shelf. I said, "Sure, I had a great career," but when I look back, you know, the money is great, but I think the greatest thing we do in order to show our appreciation is to pave the way for the young people we care about because we do have problems in this country.... So I think all of us need to take stock in ourselves and say, "Yes, play baseball, basketball, football, whatever it may be, but the greatest thing we can show our young people is that we care about them and let them grow up to be someone we can be very proud of." ... That's why I care about not the home runs, not the runs batted in, not the slugging percentage—that didn't mean as much as it does when I see a young person moving up in his education, trying to be somebody.

Thousands watched and listened in 1994 when Henry Aaron spoke at
Carson Park stadium. He broke into the minor leagues on the same field in 1952.
(Dan Reiland photo, courtesy of the *Eau Claire Leader-Telegram*)

Henry Aaron was a skinny eighteen-year-old shortstop when he came to
Eau Claire in 1952 and a national sports hero when he returned in 1994.

(David Joles photo, courtesy of the *Eau Claire Leader-Telegram*)

A few days later I called Aaron for a newspaper story, and he reflected on that afternoon in the stadium. His baseball life had flashed before his eyes that day because it had begun at Carson Park, where he symbolically crossed the railroad tracks of Mobile into a white society for the first time. Aaron was moved. "It was a great occasion," he said, "but I was sad in a way. I started thinking about playing for a little city like Eau Claire many, many years ago. I wished I could turn the clock back." He felt like a ghost, he said, standing on the same field where he broke into the minors. All his dreams had been realized, and the pursuit of Ruth's record was two decades old and fading into history. Even what Aaron calls his greatest baseball accomplishment, being inducted into the Baseball Hall of Fame, was twelve years in the past. He realized that most of a lifetime had passed since he walked to Carson Park's home plate on June 14, 1952, and hit a single.

THE END OF AARON'S ERA

Five years after Aaron left Eau Claire with a smile on his face, he was the center of attention in Milwaukee. On July 20, 1999, the Brewers celebrated Henry Aaron Night by commemorating his 755th and final home run, the one he had hit twenty-three years earlier off pitcher Dick Drago of the California Angels in County Stadium. Twenty-three years was an odd anniversary to celebrate, but the stadium was due to be replaced the following year. A new stadium, Miller Park, was going up beyond center field. County Stadium was being built the year Aaron played in Eau Claire. It opened in 1953 when the Braves moved from Boston.

Aaron was more than happy to visit the place where he hit 195 home runs, including his most memorable, the eleventh-inning blast that gave the Braves the 1957 National League pennant over the Saint Louis Cardinals. It also was the place where he reached first on an infield single in his last professional at bat in 1976.

Aaron was having a good year in 1999. In addition to the twenty-fifth anniversary of his 715th home run, which elicited hundreds of stories, he celebrated his sixty-fifth birthday with a party that drew dignitaries from around the country, including President Bill Clinton, and highlighted his Chasing the Dream Foundation. Commissioner of baseball Bud Selig, an old friend and former Brewers owner, established the Henry Aaron Award for the best offensive player in the two leagues. The award had to make Aaron especially proud because, unlike Ruth, he didn't try to hit home runs until late in his career. Aaron never had 100 strikeouts in a season, but Ruth did thirteen times, including 170 whiffs one year. Aaron ranks third in history with 3,771 hits; Ruth never reached the coveted 3,000 mark. Aaron had nearly 2,900 more turns at bat than Ruth when he hit number 715, but he also accomplished a lot more. He had 722 more total bases than any other player in baseball history. "It was not fame that I sought but rather to be the best ballplayer I could be," Aaron said in his Hall of Fame induction speech.

Recognition for Aaron came from every direction. The Brewers inducted him and five others into their Negro League Wall of Fame. All the attention in 1999 showed in Aaron's wide smiles and easy manner at the news conference on July 20. Graying at the temples and wearing a gray suit, white shirt, and brown tie with beige dots, he arrived in the stadium concourse in a golf cart and sat in front of an eight-foot-high picture of County Stadium, a home run king in his kingdom as the media sat on white plastic chairs and sought his wisdom. In regard to the end of County Stadium, the only stadium the Milwaukee Braves and Brewers had ever known, he said, "I have a love affair with this ballpark. I started my professional career in the state of Wisconsin, in Eau Claire. I was one of the first athletes who came through the organization that the ball club could claim as its own." On the subject of the record-breaking Sammy Sosa–Mark McGwire home run chases in 1998 and 1999: "It brings back some sad memories." On playing in Milwaukee versus a larger city: "If I came up in New York City, I don't know if I would have made it with all the pressure." On being bitter about the lack of respect he has received as the home run champion: "People say I'm bitter. I'm not bitter. I like to tell the truth, and sometimes that hurts. I like to see what baseball has done for minorities. I don't think it has been totally fair." On hitting forty more home runs after he broke Ruth's record: "The body had had it. The last few years got to be very tough for me."

Down the concourse from the news conference, a modest display of Aaron memorabilia was encased in glass, including a fielding glove and a pair of his baseball shoes. When Miller Park opened April 5, 2001, a seven-and-a-half-foot bronze statue of Aaron in his familiar hitting stance was dedicated outside the stadium; a statue of Brewers Hall of Famer Robin

Yount was unveiled the same day. The ball from Aaron's most famous hit—home run number 715—was in Milwaukee but not where any baseball fan might expect to find it. Ball number 715 (as well as number 714, number 755, and the ball from Aaron's first homer in 1954) can be seen at a downtown Arby's restaurant a short drive from Miller Park. The fast-food joint is one of several in the state owned by Hank Aaron Enterprises. The ball, worth six figures, is beneath a "Hank Aaron Hall of Fame" sign and part of a cardboard cutout of a beef sandwich. Bats, a jersey, and photos are included in the exhibit, along with the ball from Stan Musial's 3,000th hit. Musial was one of Aaron's childhood idols.

Henry Aaron's accomplishments mean different things to different people. In the Brewers locker room before the game that night against the Chicago White Sox, catcher Dave Nilsson said that while growing up in Australia he knew who Babe Ruth was but not Henry Aaron. Nilsson surmised that Ruth had more of an impact on the game than Aaron. Maybe that was true for whites. Ruth didn't mean much to blacks, who couldn't play while Ruth was active. Brewers center fielder Marquis Grissom grew up in Atlanta, idolized Aaron as a boy, and still does. "He's definitely one of my heroes. He means everything to me besides my dad," Grissom said, referring to how he modeled himself after Aaron and took Aaron's advice. "He's a Jackie Robinson–type person to me, what he went through to get to the big leagues and what he did." Aaron has been called a 1970s Jackie Robinson because he was the first black player to reach 3,000 hits and the first to break a major baseball record held by a white man. He also suffered some of the same indignities as Robinson along the way. Aaron represents the end of an era: He was the last of the Negro League players in the majors when he retired in 1976.

LAUGHINGSTOCK OF THE LEAGUE

For Eau Claire, Aaron symbolizes the best of the minor league baseball era in city history, a history that included another famous Milwaukee Brave and teammate of Aaron's, Bob Uecker. Although he was just one year younger than Aaron, the Milwaukee-born Uecker didn't reach the Major Leagues until 1962 and was gone by 1967. Much like Wes Westrum, he was known for his catching and not his hitting. Uecker's career totals: 146 hits, 14 home runs.

After he retired, Uecker became famous for his ability to joke about his .200 career batting average and other baseball inadequacies. He also took up radio work and was preparing for about his 5,000th Brewers broadcast on Henry Aaron Night when I found him coming out of the locker room. He looked businesslike and straight-faced, the same way he approached his deadpan comedy routines. When I asked for an interview about his Eau Claire days, he suggested we meet during the third inning when he would be temporarily off the air. Then he strode off to his booth in the press box, walking square-shouldered in his dress slacks, banded-collar shirt, and leather loafers *Miami Vice*–style without the socks.

At that moment Uecker didn't look or seem like a funny guy, but one of his ex-teammates from Eau Claire assured me he was. Uecker played parts of two years, 1956 and 1957, of Class C ball in Eau Claire. His teammates loved it. "Uecker had everybody in the dugout on the floor laughing, and that's no kidding. He was constantly cutting himself up," said Doug Smith, a first baseman. "It came so quickly to his mind, and he'd get the other team going too. We all had him pegged for TV."

Catcher Bob Uecker started his pro baseball career with the Eau Claire Braves in 1956. Even in the minor leagues, he is remembered more for his jokes and pranks than his base hits.

(Photo courtesy of the *Eau Claire Leader-Telegram*)

Smith wasn't surprised when Uecker began appearing on the *Tonight Show* with Johnny Carson many years later, but he was surprised the night Uecker mentioned Smith's name on national television. Carson asked Uecker about the longest home run he ever saw. Uecker said it was hit by Doug Smith of the Eau Claire Braves. During the season, he said, Smith got married and went on a honeymoon. On his first time at bat after the honeymoon, on his first swing—this is no lie—he hit a ball that was still rising when it went over Carson Park's left field fence at 320 feet. The ball then cleared the 160-foot width of the adjoining football field and the sidelines and then went into the football stands. "A policeman at the ballpark was checking the football stadium. He found the ball in the seventh row of the football stands. It was estimated at 650 feet," Smith said. The ball went one-eighth of a mile, which must be the definition of a "country mile," the term used by baseball old-timers when a ball was hit out of sight.

Before meeting Uecker at the Brewers–White Sox game, I had found lineup inserts for two 1956 Eau Claire Braves games against the Winnipeg Goldeyes. One of them showed Uecker uncharacteristically hitting .400 and the other showed .360, the latter indicating that he was leading the league in hitting but, as was Uecker's luck, didn't have enough official at bats to qualify. When Uecker left the airwaves for a couple of innings and began munching nuts casually in the back of the press box, apparently paying little attention to the game, he was a little surprised to hear that he once led the Northern League in hitting. "It must have been opening day," he said straight-faced, eliciting a few chuckles from press box attendants.

He remembered Eau Claire as being a fun and funny place to play. "I lived with a nice family not far from the park. I paid twenty-five dollars a week. You had to be home by a certain time or they would lock the doors. It was a lot of laughs. The worse the conditions the more you laughed. If somebody dropped a Lifesaver on the floor, there was a fight for it," Uecker said, his back to the ballgame being played below. "You got three dollars a day meal money. We bought a big piece of bologna and couple loaves of bread. It was all we could afford. I don't know if I ever enjoyed anyplace more than Eau Claire." Uecker learned more than how to play catcher in Eau Claire. He learned that with his self-deprecating humor he could be his own meal ticket in years to come. He learned, while living on bologna, that he could make a living off baloney.

In his second year at Eau Claire, Uecker struggled at the plate, going hitless in his first thirty-five or fifty times at bat, a monumental dry spell that would have lasted ten to twelve games. He wasn't just 0-for-10; he was at least 0-for-10 games. He finally broke the string with a grand slam home run against Wausau, Wisconsin. The problem might have been the bats that the Bears used. When the team ran low on bats, they would go downtown to a drugstore owned by a team official and purchase them off the racks. "That's true. They were Louisville Sluggers, but we bought them off the racks," Uecker said. Of course, those were the same bats Aaron used to hit .336 in Eau Claire.

These days, Uecker is listed in the *Marquis Who's Who of America*, along with Aaron. In addition to his six-year career in the majors, he announced *Monday Night Baseball* on ABC from 1976 to 1982, wrote a book, *Catcher in the Wry*, costarred on the TV comedy *Mr. Belvedere*, was in three *Major League* comedy movies, and made more than one hundred appearances on the *Tonight Show* with Johnny Carson. He also starred in dozens of Miller Lite beer commercials. He has been on the Baseball Hall of Fame ballot for many years—as an announcer, not a player—and most likely will be enshrined along with baseball's all-time greats.

All this from a man who had this to say about his baseball career: "I had slumps that lasted into the winter.... Sporting goods companies pay me not to endorse their products.... In 1962, I was named Minor League Player of the Year. It was my second season in the Bigs.... I knew when my career was over. In 1965, my baseball card came out with no picture.... Anybody with ability can play in the big leagues. But to be able to trick people year in and year out the way I did, I think that was a much greater feat."

In 2001 he was named to the National Radio Hall of Fame. Uecker is more famous than most of the Brewers players—has been for many years—so the team gave away Uecker bobblehead dolls to the first ten thousand fans at a 2001 game, an honor usually reserved for star players. "Maybe there's a lot of great players who weren't willing to bobble their heads the way I was. Sitting in front of a photographer, to get the pictures to make the molds, for me to sit there for hour upon hour and bobble my head up and down and wiggle it from side to side. I was sore for about a week and a half after that," Uecker said.

In 1956 and '57, he would have been listed among "Who's a Nut" in Eau

Claire. In 1956 Uecker roomed with Bears teammate Frank Benevides, who saw the budding comedian in action more than once. "Uecker got a signing bonus of sixteen thousand dollars. He bought this big blue Cadillac and drove it to Eau Claire. One time we were driving through the roads of Carson Park. Uecker said, 'Frank, get down. Get down.' I didn't know what he was up to so I got down. Then Uecker slid down so that his head was below the seat and the only thing showing was his hands on the wheel. I realized there was a cop car behind us. He couldn't see anybody driving the car. He pulled us over. It was Officer Jackson. Everybody knew Officer Jackson. He came up to the car and said, 'Oh, I should have known it was you two characters.'"

On another occasion, Benevides and three other Eau Claire players agreed after a night game to get to bed early and meet at 4 A.M. outside of Branstad Drug to go fishing at a nearby lake in Augusta, Wisconsin. The four met as planned, but Uecker also showed up "in black silk pants, a white silk shirt, and alligator shoes. He had been out all night. Uecker said, 'Where are you guys going?'" The fishermen told Uecker he wasn't dressed for the occasion, but he disagreed and became the fifth pole. As they waited for a bite in their boats, they whispered back and forth so they wouldn't scare the fish. Uecker quietly joined in the banter. "Have any bites yet?" Suddenly, one of the players said he did have a bite. With that news, the nattily attired Uecker leaped from the boat into the water and began splashing around. "You never knew what he was going to do," Benevides said.

Benevides also recalled the time he and Uecker went out for a steak dinner when the Braves were playing in Saint Cloud. "Uecker said, 'No matter what I do, Frank, keep your mouth shut.' I said, 'Bob, what are you up to now? Don't do anything that will embarrass us.' We ordered two steaks. When they arrived, Uecker wouldn't touch his. He said to the waitress, 'How come my friend has a bigger steak than me?' The waitress assured the stone-faced Uecker that his steak was the same size as Benevides's. Uecker replied, 'I'm sick and tired of people discriminating against me just because I have a big nose. I'm going to call the Better Business Bureau. I want to see the management!' After a big discussion, she came back with bigger steaks."

Uecker loved to needle opposing batters and the umpires with distracting remarks like "Hey, ump, get home. We just got a call that your wife is missing and has been seen with another umpire." He showed up for batting practice one day wearing a straw hat, long underwear, and bib overalls—because that's what mistakenly was put in his clothes bag after the team uniforms were laundered. "He got into the batter's box in that outfit and started swinging," Benevides said, shaking his head and smiling at the memory of it.

Uecker, who divorced for the second time in 2001, was a newlywed when he played in Eau Claire. He often talked about his first wife to his teammates. One time, Uecker, Benevides, and other players went into Ray's Place, a family-run bar on Water Street about a mile from the stadium. The players were sitting at the back of the long, narrow establishment when a beautiful young woman walked in. She was accompanied by a large, muscular man. The ballplayers all had their eyes on the woman. "Uecker says, 'Would you look at that. Watch this. I'm going over there and plant a kiss on her.' We told Bob not to do it, that he was only asking for trouble and might get himself killed. She was sitting at the bar. He goes over and taps her on the shoulder. She turns around. He kissed her and was mugging the hell out of her when the big guy gets up. We knew what was about to happen so we ran over there to help Uecker. Turns out it was his wife. He had set the whole thing up," Benevides said.

Benevides grew up in Fall River, Massachusetts, tried out for the Braves in 1949 at old Braves Field in Boston, signed, and played two years in the minors before serving in the Korean War. He was twenty-three when he got out of the service and came to Eau Claire. He and his wife, Pat, whom he met in Eau Claire, settled in Greenfield near Milwaukee, where he was a teacher and baseball coach for thirty-two years. He was inducted into the state high school baseball coaching hall of fame. Like Uecker, he never left Wisconsin. In 2000 Benevides moved back to Eau Claire, renewed old friendships, watched baseball games, and continued to conduct baseball clinics around the Midwest.

Another of Uecker's teammates in Eau Claire was left-handed pitcher Robert E. Lee. In 1955 Lee signed for four thousand dollars with the Braves and spent 1956 in the Pony League in Wellsville, New York. Lee met up with Uecker in 1957 in Evansville, Indiana, in the Three-I League, but by summer they both were in Eau Claire playing for manager Gordy Maltzberger. Lee planned to replace Warren Spahn in the Braves lineup, but he never made it out of the minor leagues because of control problems and a shoulder injury. Lee wound up in the plumbing business and owned the Kenosha Twins minor league team from 1984 to 1991. Lee's inability to throw strikes in Eau Claire occasionally brought Uecker out to the mound. "He would take the mask off and say, 'Did you see the good-looking chick behind home plate? Is she with anybody?' I'd say, 'I don't know, Bob. I haven't been looking.' He'd say, 'Well, take a look next time.'" Uecker was a great defensive catcher and had a powerful arm, Lee said, occasionally using it to throw a bullet back to the mound to wake up an ineffective pitcher.

Lee called Uecker unpredictable, although he was often Uecker's setup man for jokes. Uecker did an impersonation of singer Marty Robbins and the song "A White Sport Coat." Once, when Uecker wasn't in the lineup, he took bets from fans through the backstop fence that Lee, who had a ninety-mile-per-hour fastball, would strike out a certain number of people. Uecker won, of course. Late in the 1957 season, the Bears were playing in Duluth's Wade Stadium, not far from the city's skid row. It was the last road trip of the season so Uecker convinced Lee to come with him to a nickel beer bar. The two players took a pocketful of nickels and told all the homeless men on the street that they were buying. "We filled up the place. You couldn't get anybody else in there," Lee said.

Henry Aaron Night at County Stadium in 1999 featured pregame ceremonies that feted Aaron. After the game began, he joined Uecker in the radio booth, adjacent to the press box, for a couple innings of friendly banter about their baseball pasts. The media could see Aaron laughing and joking with Uecker, but with a glass window in between they could hear what was said only over the radio broadcast in the snack area. Most media paid no attention to the two laughing as they charted the game.

UECKER: "Grissom lets the ball get by in center. The runner scores."
AARON: "Remember when you had to catch four straight games?"
UECKER: "I did. [Starting catcher] Joe Torre had a broken leg. I went from a size seven and a quarter hat to like a four. I had to catch back-to-back doubleheaders."
AARON: "Remember we used to play split doubleheaders?"
UECKER: "We'd play one at eleven o'clock, catch a nap and a hot dog, and come back and play another. I think we had more fun back then. I really do."

. . . .

"Some of the balls hit today are unbelievable home runs. We had the opportunity last year to watch one of McGwire's five-hundred-plus jobs. He hit one off the scoreboard in center above where that bird flies up there. I know the balls are harder, the covers are harder, or they're using horses that are better runners or something."

AARON: "At the All-Star Game the other night I have never seen balls crushed further, harder than the ones McGwire hit. I just don't know how a ball can be hit that far. Baseballs are not meant to be hit that far."

UECKER: "No. They're like golf balls.

"A swing and a base hit to center by Grissom, and the Brewers have a runner.

"Some of those great Negro League teams, the players belonged in the minor leagues and the big leagues long before they did. Do you remember they used to do the phantom infield? Those players—as a kid, every chance I had the opportunity to go watch a game at Borchert Field [in Milwaukee]. They played on Sunday afternoons.

"Here's a smash past Ray Durham. Grissom goes to third, and the Brewers have two runners."

AARON: "I played in that league about three and a half months. I often tell this story. That league can humble you a little bit. My base salary was two hundred fifty dollars a month. I got two dollars a day meal money. I had a friend. The two of us would buy a large jar of peanut butter. I'm talking about peanut butter, not the kind you buy now. It would take two people to stir it up. I mean we would live on peanut butter and no jelly. Many nights, Bob, many a night, this is the truth, that peanut butter would get halfway down my throat. It would choke me. I tell people I have no regrets. I was humbled. I was eighteen years old. You know, being eighteen years old you do anything."

UECKER: "I have this story. Back when there was such a separation between black people and white people and black players and white players. I mean, there was never that on the team as I was introduced to it in the minor leagues. I remember in the minor leagues we would stop at particular restaurants knowing [the black players wouldn't be allowed to] go in there to eat but we did, only to aggravate people. We knew what was going to happen. But the story that always gets me is when we were staying in Bradenton, Florida. We stayed at a motel, and you stayed at a rooming house."

AARON: "Mrs. Gibson's."

UECKER: "That's right. Mrs. Gibson's rooming house. All of us had a curfew at midnight or eleven o'clock. We ate garbage food at the hotel. Mrs. Gibson's rooming house was some ways from where we stayed at this hotel. Hank and all those [black] guys all had home-cooked food and no curfew. We were checked in every night! But those guys just kept saying how bad they had it at the rooming house."

AARON: [laughs]

UECKER: "Oh, man, we had some beautiful times back then. We really did.

"You know, I've seen you hit a lot of home runs. I think the one that sticks out the most in the minds of people here is the one hit off of Billy Muffet, here at County Stadium."

AARON: "I've always said that was to me the greatest moment in my career."

UECKER: "I can see that. I can see it. That whole scenario with you rounding the bases and everyone beating up on you and swarming you. What did you hit, a slider?"

AARON: "It was a breaking ball. I think to me that was a greater moment than when I rode back to Mobile with my first car. I got it from Bud Selig."

[They both laugh after Uecker wonders whether or not Aaron paid for the car.]

UECKER: "That home run to me sticks out here as such a big part of baseball history in Milwaukee. That propelled you guys to the world championship, which I thought you guys should have won a couple of more. I really do.

"I won't keep you any longer, Henry. It's always great to see you. You know that. Henry Aaron. Nobody better folks. Nobody better."

AARON: "Thank you very much. It's been nice."

Aaron, escorted by Brewers officials—he seems to have a small entourage of guides or friends wherever he makes appearances—takes the catwalk to the mezzanine for another interview, this time on the Midwest Sports Channel, a cable station that is broadcasting the game. Uecker continues to reminisce. "He's a really good individual. He's fun. A lot of people don't know that he's really a lot of fun. We had some laughs. Henry was telling the story about that rooming house, Mrs. Gibson's. It was next to a funeral home. They got one of the guys inebriated one night and laid him in a casket. They called his wife and told her that something happened. Yeah, that was . . . [laughter]"

I headed back to Eau Claire, taking one last look at the lights of the stadium from Interstate 94. Although the Brewers would play at County

Stadium in 2000 (a construction accident that killed three workers
delayed the completion of Miller Park until 2001) this was my last visit.
A thunderstorm made the driving difficult, and the darkness and rain
pounding on the windshield seemed to block out everything but memories of the old ballpark, the unmistakable smell of which was a potpourri
of foaming beer, crushed peanut shells, steamed hotdog buns, spicy grilled
bratwurst, and moist concrete. I remember listening to Uecker when the
Brewers came to Milwaukee in 1970 while I played basketball in my backyard in La Crosse, Wisconsin, where I grew up in the 1970s. On family
trips, I tuned in to Uecker on the car radio, and on summer nights I lay
on the living room floor with my ear to the speakers of my father's beloved
hi-fi console. I remember once hitting the Montgomery Ward refrigerator
in anger when the Brewers lost a big lead in the ninth inning because
relief pitcher Frank Linzy's sinker pitch wasn't sinking. Yet my brother,
John, who was one year older, and I were apathetic fans compared with
Ron Pierzina, an adult neighbor who almost never missed a Uecker broadcast. Ron would take a transistor radio to work, holding Uecker and Merle
Harmon, Uecker's early years broadcast partner, to his ear while making
industrial air-conditioning units at Trane Company in La Crosse. If Ron
wasn't at the game on opening day he would take the big day off to have
a one-man tailgate party in his yard. His accoutrements included a pastel-
striped nylon folding lawn chair, a cooler stocked with Old Style beer—
one of them always open and in a foam-insulated holder—bratwurst on
the grill, and Bob Uecker on the air. A perfect spring afternoon, even if it
was fifty-three degrees with a cool north wind.

Most of the time the Brewers had losing seasons, but the excitement
of having big league players in Wisconsin made each day of the summer
just a little more exciting, much the way Eau Claire baseball fans must
have felt when their Bears and Braves were playing for the Northern
League championship. For many years the Brewers players weren't much
better than the Bears with the likes of Sixto Lezcano, Bobby Coluccio,
Dave May, Ron Theobald, Johnny Briggs, Bill Travers, Jerry Augustine,
and many others who never approached stardom. Uecker just made them
sound exciting. The players started to improve in the mid-1970s with the
additions of George Scott, Cecil Cooper, Don Money, a veteran named
Henry Aaron, and a rookie shortstop named Robin Yount.

Yount was midway through his rookie season in 1974 when I saw my first professional baseball game, on August 9 at County Stadium. It was four months after Aaron's record-breaking 715th home run. I was sixteen, and my older brother, John, some friends, and I drove to Milwaukee in John's four-passenger, pale yellow 1970 Mustang fastback that could do one hundred miles per hour without a sweat. Our parents never took us to games as kids, mostly because they grew up in Iowa, never went as kids, and weren't baseball fans. But when we were old enough to drive, we were there, ordering and paying for our own tickets and arranging the whole trip. I can still picture us staring wide-eyed for the first time at the emerald diamond. We were amazed at the agility and arm of the rookie shortstop, not to mention the fact that he was eighteen, about our age. The Brewers got clobbered, 13–3, by the Kansas City Royals as veteran Orlando Cepeda drove in five runs. Cepeda was getting one last chance to play in the majors after the Royals signed him from the Mexican League. I didn't know it at the time, but Cepeda was in the last year of a great career. He was the National League Rookie of the Year in 1958 with the San Francisco Giants and the National League's first unanimous Most Valuable Player in 1967 with the Saint Louis Cardinals. At that Brewer game in 1974, I had seen the last year and the first year of two baseball stars who would meet again twenty-five years later in Cooperstown. In 1999 Cepeda and Yount were inducted into the Hall of Fame. In 1974 I knew almost nothing about Orlando Cepeda, especially not the fact that he started his career in the Northern League at Saint Cloud, Minnesota, in 1956. Cepeda had played some of his earliest pro games in my home-town at Carson Park.

On the way home from the game, we stopped in Wisconsin Dells to eat leftover bologna and mustard sandwiches in a roadside park, a meal Uecker and Aaron could appreciate. Working for about $2.25 an hour at a local pizza joint, we didn't have enough money left to go to a restaurant. Someone turned on the car radio in the dark. We had been tuned in to baseball all day, and then we finally heard the news that was sweeping the nation: President Nixon had resigned. With empty pockets, we drove home thinking the news about Nixon was sad, partly because Nixon finally had gotten us out of Vietnam, assuring we wouldn't be drafted, to the eternal joy of our mothers. But Nixon's last day in office wasn't sad enough to negate what had been a great first in our lives. We still talked baseball and listened to eight-track tapes in the final two hours of the drive home, the vision of County Stadium still in our heads, not the image most other people saw when they went to bed that night, that of Richard Nixon with a recalcitrant smile, waving goodbye from the steps of a helicopter as he left Washington, D.C. When I left County Stadium for the last time on July 20, 1999, I knew that history would not repeat itself: President Clinton had already been impeached a few months earlier. He had no plans to resign.

Aaron said goodbye to County Stadium on September 28, 2000, when the Brewers played their final home game of the season, a loss to the Cincinnati Reds. Much of the retractable roof of new Miller Park already was in place beyond the center-field bleachers. After the game, Aaron and other Milwaukee Braves, Milwaukee Brewers, and Green Bay Packers heroes were introduced one by one and ran onto the field during an emotional farewell ceremony. Then Uecker gave an elegant stadium eulogy, and the stadium lights were turned off for the last time. County Stadium was history.

THE LAST OF THE SUMMER

Aaron's career and construction on County Stadium began simultaneously in 1952. That year, as the stadium went up in Milwaukee, Aaron was a runaway winner as the Rookie of the Year in the Northern League in Eau Claire. Aaron received seventy-five points in voting among sportswriters, managers, and umpires, more than the combined total points for the next three vote-getters. Runner up with twenty-seven points was Superior pitcher Alfredo Ibanez, a Cuban who had a sparkling 18-4 record with a 2.26 earned run average.

Befitting the times, the *Leader* carried a story by the Associated Press about the Rookie of the Year and identified Aaron as a "colored shortstop" for Eau Claire. It went on to say that "Aaron is the third of his race" to win the honor in Northern League history, all three being from Eau Claire. The others were Billy Bruton in 1950 and Horace Garner in 1951. Eau Claire was gaining a reputation for producing great ballplayers, and years later Aaron rightfully took offense to the fact that his color was part of the story along with his accomplishment. The Associated Press story probably had been written at one of the state AP bureaus, so it wasn't the *Leader*'s decision to highlight the color of the players, although the newspaper's sports wire editor that night easily could have edited out the reference. The *Forum* in Fargo, North Dakota, carried the same story with the same references to color. Two years after Bruton broke the color barrier in Eau Claire, black players still were news because they were black.

Duluth's Joe Caffie, a twenty-one-year-old batting champion, received the Northern League's Most Valuable Player award. As the season came to a close, the batting race came down to Aaron and Caffie, two former Negro League players from Alabama. On August 22 Aaron still led the league in hitting at .350 to Caffie's .342 average, but he slowly lost ground to Caffie in the last ten days. With seven games to play, he led Caffie .343 to .340 but then went through a 1-for-13 stretch that allowed Caffie to edge him out .342 to .336.

Caffie was born 150 miles northeast of Aaron in Ramer, Alabama, and grew up in Warren, Ohio, where he caught the eyes of scouts with his blazing speed. He could run from home to first base in three seconds flat, as fast as anyone in baseball—the minors or the majors. He wasn't bad getting on the bases either as he also led the Northern League in hits (171), total bases (271), triples (18), and runs (105). It was the first time since 1939 that a Duluth player won the batting title; in 1939, the Dukes' Robert Schmidt set a league record that never was broken with a .441 average.

In 1952 Caffie, a right fielder, was in his second season in the minor leagues, both with Duluth. In the end his speed wasn't enough; he played just forty-four games in the Major Leagues with the Cleveland Indians in 1956 and '57 before going back to the minor leagues for good. Caffie, nicknamed Rabbit, was fast, but the Dukes' Dick Newberry led the league in stolen bases with thirty-six, was second to Caffie with fifteen triples, and hit a solid .307.

Aaron finished the regular season the way he began it, with a memorable day against Saint Cloud. On September 1 Aaron was 7-for-9 against the Rox at Carson Park, as the Bears swept a season-ending doubleheader. In the second game, with the score tied 9–9 in the ninth inning, Aaron tripled with one out and scored the winning run. In the first game, Rox manager Charlie Fox tried to cool off Aaron by ordering a brushback pitch to move him off the plate. The Rox pitcher threw the ball within two inches of Aaron's nose, but Aaron swung anyway and doubled to left-center field. Fox threw up his hands and said, "I give up." Aaron hit .377

for the season against the Rox and made a believer out of old pro Charlie Fox—and a lot of other people.

Statistically, Aaron had a sound year at bat for the Bears. In 87 games, he had 116 hits and drove in 61 runs. If he had played a full 162-game Major League season, he was on pace to have 215 hits and 113 RBIs, standards of excellence. He stole 25 bases, tying the speedy Caffie for fourth in the league. In his Major League career, Aaron became known as a deceptively fast runner, one who could steal a base when he had to. Aaron committed 35 errors, ranking him fifth worst in fielding percentage among seven regular shortstops.

Still a maturing teenager, Aaron wasn't much of a home run threat. He hit nine home runs for the Bears, tying him for nineteenth place in the Northern League, well behind Fargo-Moorhead's Frank Gravino, who was first with 32 despite playing just 94 games (he was out the final month of the season). Gravino was a triple threat. He also led the league with 108 runs batted in and was eleventh best in batting at .311.

Surprisingly, the popular and powerful Wes Covington received only one first-place vote for Rookie of the Year and finished far down in the voting. Covington finished fourth in batting at .330 and had 99 RBIs and 24 home runs, including 4 grand slams. He played in 108 games, 21 more than Aaron. Covington appeared to have two weaknesses. First, with 10 errors he ranked only thirteenth in fielding percentage among the 20 outfielders who played more than 70 games that season. Second, Covington wasn't as good of a contact hitter as Aaron; he struck out in 16 percent of his at bats and Aaron just 5 percent. Aaron whiffed just 19 times in 345 trips to the plate, one of the lowest averages in the league. Already Aaron was showing the type of consistent contact hitter he would become.

To Covington's credit, however, he showed what he was made of in August when he returned from his serious head injury and went back into the batter's box unfazed. "He really took one on the mush. A lot of players were gun-shy after a hit like that, but after he came back he hit [the ball]. He really impressed me," Bears pitcher Ken Reitmeier said. Covington was hitting .335 before the concussion and maintained nearly the same average the rest of the season.

The Bears finished the season in third place at 72-53, ten games behind the pennant-winning Superior Blues, but they played well enough to make the playoffs. The top four teams qualified for the Northern League play-offs. In the semifinals it was Superior versus Eau Claire and second-place Sioux Falls versus fourth-place Duluth.

In the playoff opener at Superior on September 4, although Aaron hit a two-run home run, Eau Claire lost 5–4 in twelve innings. Eau Claire took game two with a five-run rally in the eighth inning, winning 8–7. Julie Bowers hit a three-run home run as the Bears overcame a 7–0 deficit; Aaron had two hits. Superior won the deciding game, 4–3. In his last game as an Eau Claire Bear, Aaron was hitless in four at bats.

Superior then swept Sioux Falls for the Northern League championship. The Blues' success mirrored a strong year for the Northern League. Attendance was up 22,000 from the previous season to 513,959. It would be higher than that only one more time, 518,281 in 1954.

In addition to great performances by Aaron, Caffie, Covington, and Gravino, a young pitcher from Sioux Falls named Don Elston was 18-6 and led the league in earned run average at 1.85, one of the best in league history. He had a wicked curveball and was on his way to the Major Leagues and the Chicago Cubs, although he wouldn't make it to the majors to stay until 1957. Elston and Aaron would meet again. In the majors, Aaron hit career home runs numbers 93, 131, 176, and 206 off Elston in 1957, 1958, 1959, and 1960, respectively.

Other pitchers had solid seasons. For Eau Claire, Bill Conroy was 16-9 and teenage rookie Ken Reitmeier led the team with a 3.13 earned run average. Neither made it out of the minor leagues. Reuben Stohs, the veteran Fargo-Moorhead pitcher who gave up Aaron's first home run, had a 12-9 record and 3.21 earned run average. The star pitcher of the season was righthander Gideon Applegate of Superior. He had two no-hitters, a one-hitter, two two-hitters, and two three-hitters. His record was 14-6 and he led the league with 188 strikeouts. Applegate also never made the Major Leagues.

The year he turned eighteen, Henry Aaron grew up so much that by the fall he was ready for more when most players were headed home. The end of the Northern League season wasn't the end of the season for Covington and Aaron. In the fall, Covington joined Roy Campanella's All-Stars and played outfield with another black Major League star, Larry Doby, as they barnstormed across the country. Campanella, the Brooklyn Dodgers' star catcher, was coming off an appearance in the 1952 World Series, which the Dodgers lost in seven games to the New York Yankees. After the barnstorming tour, Covington, like Bears teammate Ken Reitmeier, went into the army for two years.

After Aaron dropped off his uniform at Carson Park in September, he headed straight south. His old team, the Indianapolis Clowns, was in the Negro League World Series. They called Aaron and wondered if he would be willing to play with them again. Aaron had become a proven ballplayer and could not only hit but help put fans in the stands. Aaron caught up to the Clowns and was welcomed back. He was joined on the team by Horace Garner, the 1951 Bear who had played that season in Evansville, Indiana, in the Three-I League.

By rejoining the Clowns Aaron may have been violating his Northern League contract, which stated that he agreed not to play any postseason baseball without the consent of the team or against or with any ineligible player or team. Aaron wasn't taking a big chance, however. Because no mainstream newspapers followed the Negro Leagues it would have been hard for anyone in the Braves organization to know that the series was taking place, let alone that Aaron was playing in it.

The Clowns and the Black Barons of Birmingham, Alabama, were playing a marathon best-of-thirteen World Series across the South in Tennessee, Arkansas, West Virginia, and Alabama. It was a watered-down championship in a league that no longer mattered. It still was quality baseball, however, and it was significant to Aaron, who had grown up following Negro League ball. Aaron batted .400 and hit five home runs in the series.

One of the games was in Mobile, and it turned out to be a great homecoming for Aaron. Just seven months earlier no one had heard of him outside of his neighborhood. Now he was a minor league Rookie of the Year and playing in the Negro League World Series. It was Henry Aaron Day in Mobile, and he played on a field previously reserved for whites. He was the rising young baseball star equal to or better than all the white players he had faced that summer in the Northern League. He was a hero among the black community of Mobile but still an outcast among the white society that kept its distance from blacks in every way. Aaron was excited and disappointed to be back home. He had tasted freedom from segregation in Eau Claire, but "I went right back to a segregated society, right back into the same thing," Aaron said. The bittersweet homecoming preceded his trying 1953 season in which he helped break the color barrier at Jacksonville, Florida, in the Sally League. But he was home for the first time in nearly eight months. His high school class had graduated in the interim, and so had he, in a sense.

The Clowns went on to win the championship, but the era of the Negro League was coming to a close. By 1952 the door had swung wide open for black players. Major League teams that only five years earlier wouldn't consider signing black players were robbing the talent of Negro League teams and actually scouting black players before they could be signed by the Negro Leagues. How many more players like Willie Mays, Jackie Robinson, Henry Aaron, and Larry Doby were out there?

Halfway through the 1952 season Newberry, Caffie, Aaron, and Eau Claire pitcher Don Jordan were brought together in Eau Claire for a photograph of Northern League leaders, a sign of the changing times in baseball. Just a few years earlier, the league had no black players. Now, many of the best players were black, although they still accounted for less than a quarter of the rosters. For what it's worth, the top three Eau Claire hitters that year were the only three black men on the team: Aaron .336, Covington .330, and Julie Bowers .312.

Was the nation following baseball's lead or vice versa? In 1952 Ku Klux Klan membership was on the decline, and for the first time in seventy-one years, no lynchings were reported in the United States. Black civil rights were becoming an issue. *Brown v. Board of Education*, the school segregation case that had originated in Kansas courts, would soon be argued before the United States Supreme Court. Black voices were resonating, as evidenced by the success that year of the novel *Invisible Man*, by Ralph Ellison, who was moved to write about what it was like to be black. The people of Mobile would never have guessed that a young black baseball player nobody knew in the spring of 1952 was on his way to becoming one of the most celebrated residents in the history of their city, not to mention a hero in a white city a long way upriver. And most points between.

Sherwood Brewer was with the Kansas City Monarchs in 1952 when he first saw Aaron and thought he would be among the chosen ones despite his youthful inadequacies. "Aaron came in raw. He was hitting crosshanded and fielding ground balls with his legs crossed. But I never had any doubt about him [making it]," Brewer said. "Aaron just turned the bat over and the ball just jumped out. They tried to pitch him on the hands, wrists, and somehow he'd get on it."

Brewer spent his entire baseball career in the Negro Leagues, from 1945 through 1957, playing with the Clowns, Monarchs, and New York Cubans. Unlike Aaron, the former Negro League All-Star never had a tryout with a Major League team, but he saw many of his peers and one teammate, Ernie Banks, make it big. When the Negro Leagues folded in the late 1950s, Brewer went to work at the University of Illinois bakery, his second and only other career. Brewer, eleven years older than Aaron, retired near Chicago. "I had a lot of fun, but I didn't get rich," Brewer told me one night on the telephone, his rich, deep voice sure and steady. "I'd do it all over again. I played with and against the best ballplayers you'll ever see."

Brewer said none of the Negro League players ever doubted that they were good enough to play in the majors, but they still cheered when Robinson made it and cheered again when Aaron broke Ruth's record. Brewer was with the Clowns when Robinson broke the color barrier in Brooklyn. "When Jackie made it, it was all anybody in the Negro Leagues would talk about. It was a good feeling for all of us, and Jackie Robinson was not the best ballplayer in our league by a long shot. But we were proud of Jackie because of the way he hung in there. There was nothing in this world passive about Jackie, but he knew what he had to do to make it work. I asked him myself one time how many times he wanted to quit. He said, 'Every day.' But he would never do it. He was more upset about the [racial] trouble he had on his own ball club than with the other players in the league," Brewer said. "When Hank broke Ruth's record, I was ecstatic. He was a much better ballplayer than given credit for. He just went out and got the job done."

In his lifetime, Brewer saw baseball integrated along with America. He was born in Clarksdale, Mississippi, in 1923, but it's not the same Mississippi today. "I never dreamed I'd go to Mississippi and sit down in a restaurant wherever I pleased. I never dreamed it would happen."

Trying to reach Aaron, one of the nation's most famous sports celebrities, is almost as difficult as getting through to a president. I wanted to arrange a telephone interview to resolve some lingering questions I had about his days in Eau Claire. First I called Aaron's office in Atlanta and heard a recording from his secretary, Susan Bailey. She said that any interview or appearance requests needed to be faxed or e-mailed to her. After following procedure, I received a response by e-mail that Aaron would be able to give me ten minutes of his time in two weeks. When the day arrived, I called and learned that a conference call had come up and was asked to call back ninety minutes later. When I did that, Bailey asked if I could call back in another five minutes because Aaron then would be out of his house and in his car and she could patch me through to his cellular phone.

Suddenly, through the miracle of technology, I was talking to Aaron as he drove from his home in suburban Atlanta to his BMW dealership. At that moment I realized why Aaron is such a role model to so many people: Aaron himself is a miracle, a poor, put-down black kid from the South who became one of the nation's earliest black cultural heroes. Now he was supplying luxury cars to the upper class. We talked about Eau Claire, which usually is pronounced with the emphasis on the second syllable, "Eau CLAIRE," although Aaron always has called it "EAU Claire." He reiterated that his first year in the minors, one of only two years he spent in the minors, was crucial to his career. "I was sure of myself then as a baseball player and saw I could compete with the other players. The experience of playing every day with the competitiveness around me—I knew I could play professional baseball. The Negro League was a good league, but playing in Eau Claire, which was a professional league, to play with a lot of players more on the professional level, players who were drafted and highly thought of ..." Aaron believes he was thoroughly tested as a baseball player and as a person in Eau Claire because the competition was good, his mettle was challenged by the long road trips and often inclement weather in the Upper Midwest, and he was on his own in a strange culture for the first time. In addition, he said, Carson Park was a quality, professional-caliber stadium. He added up all the plusses and said, "The Northern League was probably one of the best leagues in all of baseball."

As our conversation continued, Aaron, then sixty-six years old, began to recall his 1952 teammates, wondering what had happened to some of them. He was closest to the two other black players on the team, John "Wes" Covington and William "Julie" Bowers. Yet he didn't know that Covington was working at a newspaper in Edmonton, and he didn't remember having seen or heard from Bowers since 1952.

Of the seventeen Bears on the team at the end of the season, only Aaron, Covington, and Johnny Goryl made it to the majors. Player-manager Bill Adair made it as an assistant coach and was in the running to become a manager in the majors more than once. Adair finally got his chance in 1970, managing ten games for the Chicago White Sox, the worst team in baseball that year with 106 losses. After two seasons in Eau Claire, the nomadic Adair, with his wife and their two young girls, moved on to coach in El Dorado, Arkansas, in the Cotton States League. Adair finally gave up coaching and scouting in the 1980s and moved back to Mobile, Alabama, where he developed Alzheimer's disease, according to his wife, Olean Adair. "At times he doesn't even remember me, and we've been married for sixty years," she said in the spring of 2000. Adair saw Aaron momentarily in the late 1990s when Aaron returned to Mobile to dedicate the city's new minor league baseball field, aptly named Henry Aaron Stadium. Bill Adair passed away June 17, 2002.

After the 1952 season, most of the Bears scattered to their homes. Johnny Goryl, Bobby Brown, Lantz Blaney, Bill Conroy, Bob MacConnell, and Julie Bowers headed east, and Chester Morgan went south. Brown gave Kornack a ride in his yellow Packard convertible as far as Brooklyn, and Kornack took a train the rest of the way to the Boston area. Several of the players would be back, however. Bowers played again with Eau Claire in 1953, and Goryl and Jordan returned to the team in 1954.

Blaney, the speedy outfielder, became a police detective and an insurance agent in Lexington, Kentucky. He retired to his hometown in Morgantown, West Virginia, and died in 1997 of a heart attack at the age of sixty-seven.

Kornack stayed in baseball only a couple more seasons before going back east for good. He went into the funeral business in 1969 and became part owner of Kraw-Kornack Funeral Home in Norwood, Massachusetts. Occasionally, he goes to flea markets and finds old baseball books with his picture in them. Of course, those books are about Aaron and the picture is of the 1952 Bears. Aaron and Kornack are in row two.

After spending 1953 and 1954 in the service, Reitmeier returned to Carson Park in 1955 to pitch for the Bears but retired from baseball with a shoulder injury in 1956. Reitmeier, who grew up in Saint Cloud, Minnesota, found a job, played semipro baseball, and remained in Eau Claire until 1962. Then he became an officer with the Scott County Sheriff's

Department in Minnesota and settled down in Shakopee, near Minneapolis. But he never forgot Eau Claire, that rookie year he played with Henry Aaron and the attractive female fan who used to shout at him to get the ball over the plate. The fan, Shirley Stolp, became his wife.

Reitmeier used to joke that he led the league only in stolen towels, but he also stole his gray 1952 Bears road jersey after that season and kept it in a box for forty-six years. In 1998 he gave the heavy wool uniform back to the city of Eau Claire to be displayed at the stadium. He presented it near the Carson Park pitching mound during a ceremony to rededicate the stadium after its renovation. Reitmeier also walked away in 1952 with his Bears socks, snapshots of his teammates (including one of a spindly Aaron standing near home plate), and autographed balls from Aaron and Covington. "I probably have one of the first Aaron autographs," he said.

Morgan, called "Collins" or "Chet" by teammates, would become a familiar face to Aaron even after 1952. In 1953 Morgan and Aaron moved up to Jacksonville in the Sally League, where Aaron played second base and Morgan centerfield. Aaron met and married Barbara Lucas in Jacksonville, and Morgan and his wife, Shirley Benedict, whom he had met the previous season in Eau Claire, were invited to the wedding. Morgan witnessed Aaron's entire minor league career. In the spring of 1954 Morgan and Aaron were at Milwaukee Braves spring training hoping to get the one open outfield spot on the roster. When Bobby Thomson broke his ankle, the roster spot went to Aaron instead of Morgan, who wasn't surprised. "Hank made big strides in every area. He put on ten to fifteen pounds and had that good year in the Southern League. He thrived on that," Morgan said. The spring of 1954 was Morgan's last real shot at the majors. He played in the minors through 1956 and retired at age twenty-five. Morgan ran a boys' camp in northern Wisconsin for six years, then spent six years in Italy coaching baseball and helping start the country's Olympic baseball program. He settled down in El Paso, Texas, where he went into the insurance business and played in an old-timers' baseball league until age sixty-five.

Morgan's dream was to follow in the footsteps of his father, Chester "Chick" Morgan, who played with the Detroit Tigers (fourteen games in 1935, when they won the World Series behind future Hall of Famers Hank Greenberg and Charlie Gehringer, and seventy-four games in 1938). Chick Morgan also was coached in the minors by Burleigh Grimes, the famous spitballer who began his minor league career in Eau Claire in 1912. The elder Morgan used five thousand dollars from his baseball salary to buy the family farm in Greenville, Mississippi, where his athletic son picked cotton with blacks and dreamed of the big leagues.

Pitcher Elmer Toth liked Eau Claire so well that he thought of staying after the season, but he couldn't find a job and moved on. He spent a total of ten seasons in the minors, playing in such places as Texas City, Texas, in the Big State League, where he was 21-7; Jackson, Mississippi; El Dorado, Arkansas; and Chattanooga, Tennessee. "I'd do it again. I liked it," said Toth. "But you got to be twenty-seven or twenty-eight and you just said, 'I've got to get a job.'" He spent the next thirty years working at the Pittsburgh-Wheeling steel mill in Allenport, Pennsylvania. In 1985 he saw Bears manager Bill Adair scouting a game in Florida, and they reminisced about their year together in Eau Claire and a second year together in Owensboro, Kentucky. They also talked about Henry Aaron, who was in the Baseball Hall of Fame by then. "He was a sharp hitter," Toth said of the Aaron he knew as a teenager.

The Boston Braves minor leaguers weren't the only ones on the move after the 1952 season. By the start of the 1953 season, they all would be property of the Milwaukee Braves after the team left seventy-six years of history (and sagging attendance) behind in New England for a new start in Wisconsin.

Aaron tried but couldn't remember many specifics about his Bears teammates, but he did remember Susan Hauck, the dark-haired, athletic girl he became friends with nearly fifty years earlier on her front porch in Eau Claire. In recent years, Aaron had tried to recall her name, especially when he was working on *I Had a Hammer*. He called Eau Claire more than once seeking information about her but had no luck, even though she had never left the city. When I told him during the interview that I had found her and that she was still living in Eau Claire, it seemed as if one piece of his Eau Claire memory had snapped into place. I sensed that through all of the home runs, the years of traveling, the countless interviews with reporters, the countless autographs for fans, he still could see her face clearly. They had both been eighteen and attracted to each other. One black. One white. He asked about her and wanted her phone number. "That was an important relationship for me, to have a family take me into their heart, to make me feel welcome," Aaron said of the Haucks.

Neither Aaron nor Hauck said they dated, but back then they went about as far as either of them dared to go—holding hands and spending a few hours at her house or with friends.

Soon after I said my goodbyes to Aaron and after he reached his BMW dealership, he placed a call to Susan Hauck. The young man and woman, whose friendship in 1952 quietly and privately symbolized the beginning of reconciliation between the South and North, between black and white America, spoke to each other for the first time in nearly fifty years. They talked about their grown children and old friends. Aaron told her he was going to Japan. Hauck told him that her husband recently had died. Aaron asked Hauck why she didn't come to Carson Park the day of the statue dedication. They recalled the night a bunch of them went by car to the lookout over Elk Mound. In a few minutes, they put fifty years behind them. Aaron still was soft spoken and friendly. Hauck still was sweet and honest. Hauck thought the international sports hero was at heart the same shy southern teenager she once knew.

Hauck was happy that he had called. Aaron was too, and he told her to call if she ever needed anything. Hauck knew that, more than anything, Aaron called out of a heartfelt and deep sense of gratitude for helping a scared, skinny kid who at times didn't know which way to turn. "He was just grateful because our family treated him without prejudice," Susan Hauck said. "Our family didn't do that much. Maybe he just felt like he was being treated equal."

BIBLIOGRAPHY

INDEX

BIBLIOGRAPHY

Aaron, Hank. *The Courage to Succeed.* Eau Claire: University of Wisconsin–Eau Claire, 1982. Videorecording.

Aaron, Hank, with Dick Schaap. *Home Run: My Life in Pictures.* Kingston, N.Y.: Total Sports, 1999.

Aaron, Hank, with Lonnie Wheeler. *I Had a Hammer: The Hank Aaron Story.* New York: HarperCollins, 1991.

Aaron, Henry. *Henry Aaron.* New York: Thomas Y. Crowell, 1968.

Barland, Lois. *Sawdust City: A History of Eau Claire, Wisconsin, from the Earliest Times to 1910.* Stevens Point, Wis.: Worzalla, 1960.

Brashler, William. *The Story of Negro League Baseball.* New York: Ticknor & Fields, 1994.

Buege, Bob. *The Milwaukee Braves: A Baseball Eulogy.* Milwaukee: Douglas American Sports Publications, 1988.

Carruth, Gordon, and associates, eds. *The Encyclopedia of American Facts and Dates.* New York: Thomas Y. Crowell, 1956.

Carver, Jonathan. *Travels through the Interior Parts of North-America, in the Years 1766, 1767, and 1768.* London: Printed for the author and sold by J. Walter, 1778.

Heward, Bill, with Dimitri V. Gat. *Some Are Called Clowns: A Season with the Last of the Great Barnstorming Baseball Teams.* New York: Thomas Y. Crowell, 1974.

Hildebrand, John. *Mapping the Farm: The Chronicle of a Family.* New York: Knopf, 1995.

Holway, John B. *Blackball Stars: Negro League Pioneers.* Westport, Conn.: Meckler, 1988.

Kahn, Roger. *The Boys of Summer.* New York: Harper & Row, 1971.

King, Martin Luther Jr. "Letter from Birmingham Jail." In *The Best American Essays of the Century,* edited by Joyce Carol Oates and Robert Atwan, 263–79. Boston: Houghton Mifflin, 2000.

Moffi, Larry. *This Side of Cooperstown: An Oral History of Major League Baseball in the 1950s.* Iowa City: University of Iowa Press, 1996.

Moffi, Larry, and Jonathan Kronstadt. *Crossing the Line: Black Major Leaguers, 1947–1959.* Jefferson, N.C.: McFarland, 1994.

Peterson, Robert W. *Only the Ball Was White.* Englewood Cliffs, N.J.: Prentice-Hall, 1970.

Plimpton, George. *Hank Aaron: One for the Record; The Inside Story of Baseball's Greatest Home Run.* New York: Bantam Books, 1974.

Ribowsky, Mark. *A Complete History of the Negro Leagues, 1884 to 1955.* Seacaucus, N.J.: Carol Publishing Group, 1995.

Sullivan, Neil J. *The Minors: The Struggles and the Triumph of Baseball's Poor Relation from 1876 to the Present.* New York: St. Martin's Press, 1990.

Thompson, William F. *The History of Wisconsin.* Vol. 6, *Continuity and Change, 1940–1965.* Madison: State Historical Society of Wisconsin, 1988.

Thorn, John, and Pete Palmer with David Reuther, eds. *Total Baseball.* New York: Warner Books, 1991.

Torre, Joe, with Tom Verducci. *Chasing the Dream: My Lifelong Journey to the World Series.* New York: Bantam, 1997.

White, Herman D. *An Informal History of the Northern Baseball League.* Saint Paul, Minn.: Gryphon Press, 1982.

INDEX